RELIGION
or
RELATIONSHIP
Which One Do You Want?

RELIGION
or
RELATIONSHIP
Which One Do You Want?

By Mark R. Anderson
www.markandersonministries.com

Published by:
Mark Anderson Ministries
P.O. Box 66
Cody, WY 82414-0066 USA
Email: goodnews@vcn.com
Phone: 307-587-0408

ISBN-13: 978-1537281599
ISBN-10: 1537281593

Book design/layout by Gabriel Arosemena, GEA-designs
Interior artwork by Marc L. Gottfried

Special acknowledgements and thanks to:

- Sharmila Anderson my lovely wife and helpmate for transposing and editing, adding many thoughts or expounding more thoroughly to this book.

- Contributing Editor- Dr. Paul Bergamini

- Rick Joyner for the life changing books of his that have had a great influence in putting the first part of this book together. We have quoted from Rick Joyner's books: The Final Quest, Overcoming the Religious Spirit, The Surpassing Power of His Greatness and the Morning Star Journal. Even though we have never met Rick Joyner, his books and teachings have had a great impact on our life and ministry starting in 1998. We feel as a result of putting into practice his teachings the anointing in our life and ministry has become much stronger. We highly recommend the above books. Many lives have been changed by the revelation in these books.

ENDORSEMENTS

"Mark's new book deals with the topic that many of the church do not want to talk about. It is the way the enemy is bringing division, to keep the church from fulfilling its call. He has done an excellent job of tackling this topic and showing how to get past it and step into the call that we have. I highly recommend this book not as a quick read but it is a necessary read. I want to encourage you to look at this topic with a new set of eyes and realize what the enemy is trying to do and move forward."

– Jim Rogers
Experiencing His Presence Ministries
www.ExperiencingHisPresence.org

"Mark lives what he preaches. His relationship with God is real. His instructions on humility and living for an audience of One are manifest in his life. I have had the honor of knowing Mark for over 25 years. He is one of God's heroes. He never quits. The call on Mark's life keeps him moving forward. He has sacrificed year after year to carry the gospel to difficult regions of the world. As you read this book, you are bathing in words that flow from his heart—a heart that has been tested and found pure."

– Harold Eberle,
President Worldcast Ministries and Publishing

"I have known Mark Anderson since he was 28 years old. He is a very no nonsense, practical, down-to-earth type of guy. That's the kind of book you're about to read. Jesus took the time to expose the phony, oppressive religious spirit of His day and contrasted it with the life-giving ways of His Kingdom. Nobody wants religion-everybody wants the God-kind of life! As you read Mark's book I believe that any remnants of the religious spirit will be replaced with the Life-giving ways of King Jesus. Happy Reading!"

– Steve C Shank is an author and Teacher/Preacher to the Nations You can get his books "God Made Visible-Seeing His Glory and Experiencing His Presence" and "Schizophrenic God?--Finding Reality in Conflict, Contradiction, and Confusion" From amazon. com or his website at SteveCShank.com

TABLE OF CONTENTS

INTRODUCTION

I love what Bono the lead singer of the rock band U2 said about Holy Spirit. *"I often wonder if religion is the enemy of God. It's almost like religion is what happens when the Spirit has left the building."* Bono nailed it. When Holy Spirit is not allowed to move freely and be in control of our lives, churches, meetings and ministries all we have is cold dead religion. This is the enemy of our great God. Your knowledge and insight into the word does not matter if all it is arrogant head knowledge and Holy Spirit is not present manifesting His power and glory. So many Christians have settled for religion with little or no relationship or intimacy with Father, Son and Holy Sprit. Sometimes they have just enough religion to inoculate themselves from a real relationship with Father, Son and Holy

Spirit.

When Jesus walked this earth the greatest opposition he faced was from religious leaders of His day, bound by a religious spirit. It is no different today. Our sins and the religious spirit are what put Jesus on the cross and crucified Him. Religion seeks to shut down Holy Spirit from moving in a powerful way to reveal Jesus to us.

Jesus did not came down from heaven to establish a new religion called Christianity. Religion is man's futile attempt to connect to God or to get to their gods. Religion will never get you to God. God Himself, Jesus the Creator did not come down to earth so we would have another religion or be religious but so we could have a personal relationship with Him. Thank God I do not have religion with with my wife Sharmila. How boring that would be. I have a relationship with her, which makes our marriage and life together so wonderful. Even more so, Jesus came so we could have relationship. Relationship with Christ and fellowship with Holy Spirt is where the power and love of God work hand in hand to reveal our Savior Jesus Christ to this lost and dying world. The religions of man will never get anyone to heaven.

Jesus came so we can have a personal relationship with Him. There is a huge difference between having religion or being religious and having a personal relationship with Jesus. Religion is not the answer. Jesus the way, the truth and life is the answer and the only way to make it to heaven and the only way to have relationship with the living God (see John 14:6).

If you look around this world and throughout history the religions of men (when bound by a religious spirit) have done more damage than good. Sad to say so-called Christians have also been part of that. How many people have been turned off to Christ and his love all because what they saw was cold dead religion and because of that they fled from Christianity. Some became fierce haters of God and became atheists. The great leader who brought freedom to India, Mahatma Ghandi read the Bible because he greatly admired the teachings of Christ. He was extremely interested in Christianity. But he never became a Christian because he could not find Christians who lived the Bible. All he probably saw was dead religion in those claiming to be Christian.

How many political leaders have used religion to control the masses to do exactly what they wanted and herd the masses as 'useful idiots' or pawns? Many times religion is used to keep them in power, even if they care less about that religion. How many pastors driven by insecurity and a religious spirit have used the Bible wrongly to control their little flocks with and an iron rod? As I travel around the world I have noticed different great moves of God and then insecure political leaders or so called Christian leaders sway the masses to turn against those who spread the Gospel of Jesus Christ. How many martyrs have shed their blood because of religion? How many wars have broken out and millions killed because of the religions of man? I am not saying only bad things have come from religion but many bad things have transpired in the world since the time of Christ because of people controlled by a religious spirit, prejudice, bias, and arrogance, all because of 'their religion.'

Throughout history religion has always persecuted those who have a relationship Christ. We can even see these things happen in the different waves of revival that have broken out in the past 125 years. Many times when a movement dies down (mainly because of arrogance) and God raises up other leaders to bring in a fresh move of God the former wave persecutes the new wave, trying to shut down what God is doing. It is the same thing each time, religion persecutes those pursuing Jesus and a close personal relationship with Him.

Other times out of arrogance just to be different and bring glory to oneself, people will rebel against a so-called religious spirit in the church. They do it in a way that only brings glory to themselves. This form of rebellion and arrogance just breeds another type of religious spirit that does not produce lasting fruit. True Christ-like humility like Jesus had brings radical change, that produces lasting change and fruit that goes right into eternity. What will you pursue religion, the status quo, what is politically correct, or relationship? In this book we want to break it down and show how religion can come in and stop us from pursuing a relationship with the living Christ. We will also show how relationship, humility, and the grace of God can bring in the supernatural, along with His glory, into our midst with great signs, wonders, and miracles from Heaven.

Different Degrees of the Religious Spirit

As we get into this teaching there are things to keep in mind. Many people are controlled by religious spirits but in differing degrees. 1- Some have no connection to Christianity but might be bound to a religious spirit from a different religion. 2- Some are connected to Christianity but have no relationship with Christ. Jesus said in Matthew 6:23 ... *If therefore the light that is in you is darkness, how great is that darkness!* 3- The third type is full gospel believers in Christ bound by a religious spirit. This is what we want to focus on in this book. Dangerous! Because true followers of Christ paint a horrible picture of Christ to the world if they do things out a critical spirit, arrogance and pride. This is the exact opposite of Christ's nature. James 4:6 says

Therefore He says: "God resists (Greek - **rages in battle against**) *the proud, But gives grace to the humble."* This kind arrogance seeks to control other followers of Christ. Sometimes their attitude is "my way or the Highway." They do not want people to question them, but instead just blindly fall in line.

We will look at all these varying degrees of the religious attitude, religious spirit and show how we can walk in victory over these.

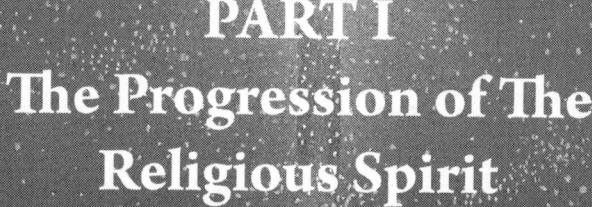

PART I
The Progression of The
Religious Spirit

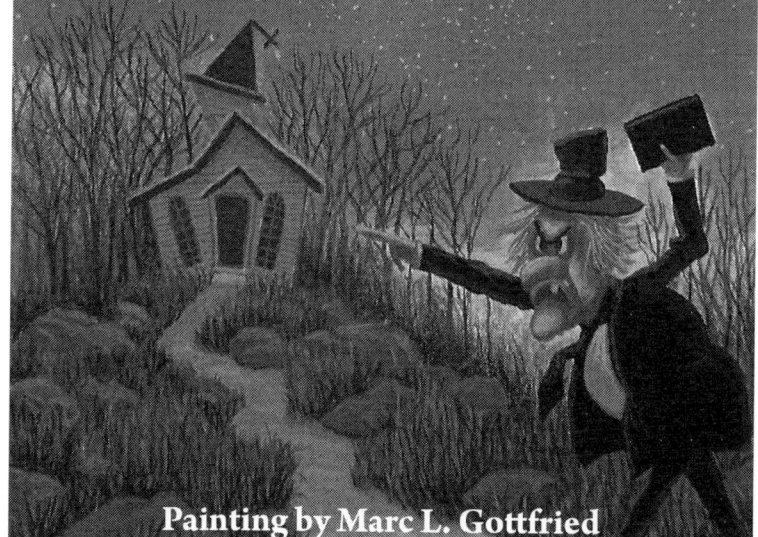

Painting by Marc L. Gottfried

CHAPTER 1

How the Religious Spirit Begins

In Part I we will cover the attitude of the religious leaders of Jesus' day and how it has been passed down through the generations to this present day. In Part II I will show the alternative to the religious spirit, relationship and what that can bring in one's life. How does the religious spirit enter into one's life? An ungodly religious attitude or religious spirit is not one that a person acquires overnight. It starts as a small seed and if left unchecked, it mushrooms and becomes a major stronghold in one's life. At this point it can go from being just an attitude to a demonic stronghold in one's life. My attempt through this book is to try to help people identify this crippling attitude and/or spirit, at its inception and deal with it, before it becomes a stronghold in one's life, ministry, or in the church.

Many years ago I was sharing at an inner city church in Buffalo, New York on the progression of the religious spirit. A black brother stood up as the message was really sinking in and shared a great revelation that resonates to this day. He shouted *"That religious spirit is a fungus among us."* He nailed it. **We need to cleanse ourselves of this fungus among us.**

Matthew 16:5-12, *"Now when His disciples had come to the other side, they had forgotten to take bread. Then Jesus said to them, 'take heed and beware of the leaven of the Pharisees and Sadducees'. And they reasoned amongst themselves, saying, it is because we have taken no bread. But Jesus, being aware of it, said to them, 'O you of little faith, why do you reason among yourselves because you have brought no bread? Do you not yet understand, or remember the five loaves of the five thousand and how many baskets you took up? Nor the seven loaves of the four thousand and how many large baskets you took up? How is it you do not understand that I did not speak to you concerning bread? -But to 'beware of the leaven of the Pharisees and Sadducees'. Then they understood that He did not tell them to beware of the leaven of bread, but of the doctrine of the Pharisees and Sadducees."*

From the above scripture verses it is very clear that Jesus is warning His disciples to beware and cautious of the teachings of the Pharisees and Sadducees; how much more pertinent is this warning for us in this day and age. If the disciples had to guard themselves from the teachings and the attitudes of the religious leaders of their day, it is imperative that we the Church of today do the same. This ungodly attitude that the religious leaders of Jesus' day had, started rather small, but as time progressed it became a major hindrance to what Jesus wanted to accomplish. These religious leaders, some of who I am sure had a great zeal for God, became a major stumbling block to others as they allowed the religious spirit to progress in their lives and control them.

Leaven is the same as yeast that is added in dough to cause it to rise when baking bread. Jesus compares the doctrines and attitude of the Pharisees to leaven used in bread (verse 12). It causes the bread to inflate but it offers no nutritional value. Similarly the religious spirit does not add to the life and power of the Body of Christ. It only inflates it.

The Pharisees and Sadducees were the religious leaders in Jesus' days. They spent hours studying the scriptures and were well grounded in it. Thus, their problem was not the lack of knowledge of scripture, rather what they did with it, and how they used it to bind people in religious chains. Their major problem was their heart attitude. They were in the grips of the stifling religious spirit.

The religious Spirit cripples people up with guilt and shame, in order to keep them bound. The devil condemns through a religious spirit but Holy Spirit convicts. Being consumed with guilt and shame will never in the long run produce lasting fruit. Allowing the Holy Spirit to convict us to deal with areas of our life will produce lasting fruit if we yield to His gentle conviction. Jesus talking of Holy Spirit said *when He has come, He will convict* (Greek- also means convince) *the world of sin, and of righteousness, and of judgment* (John 16:8).

Jesus experienced no difficulty ministering to the prostitutes, tax collectors and heathen; rather the greatest opposition He faced was from the Pharisees and Sadducees, the supposed religious leaders of the day. Today the greatest opposition to what God desires to do comes from the so-called religious people rather than the unbeliever. In Jesus' day the unfortunate and sad fact was that the religious spirit had grown to such enormous proportions, that when Jesus performed a miracle, these religious leaders wanted to kill Him. John 11 narrates the miracle of Jesus raising Lazarus from the dead. This caused the religious leaders to want to kill Him to get Him out of the way. Notice in John 11:48 their reason for wanting Him dead: *"If we let Him alone like this, EVERYONE WILL BELIEVE ON HIM..."* Think about it! A MIRACLE WORKING JESUS IS AN UNSTOPPABLE JESUS.

One of the goals of the religious spirit is to stifle the miracle working power of Jesus, thus keeping people from believing in Jesus. The effects of the religious spirit are evident all over the world today in obstructing moves of God and hindering the miracle working power of Jesus. This spirit has nothing to do with the spirit of Jesus Christ. Many will be deceived thinking that this spirit is of Jesus. Jesus said *"...He who has seen me has seen the Father..."* (John 14:9). If we want to know what Father God or Jesus God the Son is all about just look at Jesus in the Gospel accounts. A religious spirit did not bind Him. He confronted the religious leaders of His day with great authority. He walked in power, humility and unconditional love.

A great part of Jesus' ministry was healing the sick and casting out demons. 1 John 2:6 says *"He who says he abides in Him ought himself also to walk just as He walked."* We need to walk in that same kind of power and anointing. He has not stopped performing miracles and/or setting people free of demons. Hebrews 13:8 says "Jesus Christ is the same yesterday, today, and forever." Sometimes miracles and healings are what it takes to bring people into the kingdom.

Woman caught in Adultery

"But Jesus went to the Mount of Olives. Now early in the morning He came again into the temple, and all the people came to

*Him; and He sat down and taught them. Then the scribes and the Pharisees brought to Him a woman caught in adultery. And when they had set her in the midst, they said to Him, Teacher, this woman was caught in adultery, in the very act. Now Moses, **in the law, commanded us that such should be stoned.** But what do you say? This they said **testing Him, that they might have something of which to accuse Him.** But Jesus stooped down and wrote on the ground with His finger, as though He did not hear. So when they continued asking Him, He raised Himself up and said to them, 'He who is without sin among you, let him throw a stone at her first.' And again He stooped down and wrote on the ground. Then those who heard it, being convicted by their conscience, went out one by one, beginning with the oldest even to the last. And Jesus was left alone, and the woman standing in the midst. When Jesus had raised Himself up and saw no one but the woman, He said to her, 'Woman, where are those accusers of yours? Has no one condemned you?' She said, No one, Lord. And Jesus said to her, '**Neither do I condemn you; go and sin no more.**"* (John 8:1-11).

Here a women was caught in the act of adultery. What about the man? Why was he not brought before Jesus for judgment? Jesus said he who is without sin should cast the first stone. He then stooped down and wrote on the ground. I wonder what He wrote? It said they were all convicted and left one by one. What about Jesus? He was without sin. He could have cast the first stone. That is not the way Jesus acted, then or now. He is a God of great love. He forgives and forgets. He separates the sin from the sinner and sees our future and what we will become. **To Jesus it does not matter so much what you have done but what you will become.**

Once while ministering in Nicaragua I heard of a couple that had just accepted Christ. They attended a local church hoping to learn more about Jesus. Before they got a chance to know more about Jesus, the pastor and leaders in that church kicked them out of the church. The reason? They were not married, but living together in sin. What would have happened if they had been more patient with them, and let that couple stay in the church instead of embarrassing them. They could have preached about who they could be in Christ, showed them the love and goodness of God. Romans 2:4 says ... *"the goodness of God leads you to repentance."* These two would have been convicted of their sin, repented, and gotten married. Then they would have been in a position to serve Jesus. Instead the church leaders' religious spirit drove the couple back into the world.

This is an example of what we have witnessed all over the world as we have conducted campaigns in many nations. The religious spirit driving people away from our loving Savior! It is a shame that sometimes Christians do not walk in patience with new converts who are still struggling with certain sins in their lives, thus driving them away from Christ! Is this how Jesus would have acted? I think not! He asked the woman caught in adultery where her accusers were. She said there were none. Jesus reveals His heart for people by saying *"neither do I condemn you, go and sin no more"* (John 8:11). Jesus did not condemn or condone her sin. He lovingly gave her an alternative to her lifestyle. What became of this woman? She became a follower of Jesus. Our former lifestyles and sins are of no consequence to Jesus once we repent. His focus is on what we can become and accomplish for His glory. My friend Mike Francen says "God never consults your past to determine your future."

I came across something posted on Facebook by Rockfeed. net written by Brian Storm on August 1, 2016 as I was putting the finishing touches on this book that fits right in with what we are addressing. **Brian 'Head' Welch lead guitarist** for the Metal Band **Korn** is taking his fame in Rock Music and using it as a platform to reach the lost for Christ. He knows what the Lord has delivered him out of. He is doing this with the love, humility and the power of Christ in the secular world. While ministering to some down and out people who attended their concerts he came under attack from a number of Christians who were bound by a religious spirit. He posted this powerful statement below:

"*Regarding my post about transgenders yesterday: Most comments were amazing, thanks. To the few people that were running their mouth about Sodom and Gomorrah and the sin of homosexuality, please open your hearts and read this carefully: God looks at the heart and man looks on the outside. What I do and what we all need to do is find out what is inside people's hearts. One of the people in the photo yesterday shared their pain and horrible abuse that happened to them that went on for years. I think another had "Christians" attack them and throw them away like trash in the past. These people and dozens of others on my tour this summer are getting some level of inner-healing. They are experiencing non-judgmental Jesus lovers who are planting seeds and speaking life into them. Some of them are having instant change, but for most of them, it's going to take some time. Many tears are being shed and their hearts are softening. Each heartless post from you judgemental ones are only helping to harden their hearts to Jesus once again.*

The Gospel of Christ isn't like fast food. Not everyone has an overnight dramatic conversion like mine. Often times the relationship with God takes hold many years or even a decade or more later. When you religious people try to force instant repentance and point out people's flaws, you are dismantling what God is trying to do inside of hearts. If I can convince even one hardhearted Christian to stop posting about instant repentance and hell fire while me and my friends are trying to love people to Jesus over time, then I guess this post was worth it.

It's a tiring job trying to persuade my people to fall in love with the Son of God, Jesus, while other "Christians" are chasing them away with their posts at the same time. I'm begging you, please stop."

You can see from the heartfelt post that Brian's heart breaks for the lost and hurting he is ministering to. Then so called Christians bound by a religious spirit chase these people away from a loving Savior they are just getting to know. How many people ready for salvation have been driven away by religious fanatics who are not passionate for Christ, but judgmental, uncaring, arrogant and bound by spirit of religion? We will address this more in the coming chapters.

Staying Free of the Religious Spirit

Mark 7:1-13 clearly and **concisely charts how the religious spirit grows and progresses,** if not repented of and dealt with at its inception. It is our desire to expose this demonic religious spirit to keep it from affecting Christians. We need to realize and accept the fact that all of us can have problems in our lives with this attitude or spirit **if** we leave our heart unchecked. A sure sign of the religious spirit is when we always think messages are for another person, and somehow never for us. The religious leaders of Jesus day had an "everybody else but me" attitude. We can never experience total freedom in Christ if we take on this attitude. We need to be Christians that **search our heart motives regularly.** So do not take this book, give it a friend and say "you really need this" without reading it yourself and searching your heart.

*"Then the Pharisees and some of the scribes came together to Him, having come from Jerusalem. Now when they saw some of His disciples eat bread with defiled, that is, with unwashed hands, **they found fault.** For the Pharisees and all the Jews do not eat unless they wash their hands in a **special way, holding the traditions** of elders. When they came from the marketplace, they do not eat unless they wash. And there are many other things, which they have received and hold, like the washing of cups, pitchers, copper vessels, and couches. Then the Pharisees and scribes asked Him, why do your disciples not walk according to the traditions of the elders, but eat bread with unwashed hands? He answered and said to them, ' well did Isaiah prophesy of you hypocrites, as it is written this people **honors Me with their lips, But their heart is far from Me. And in vain they worship Me. Teaching as doctrines the commandments of men. For laying aside the commandment of God, you hold the tradition of men**- the washing of pitchers and cups, and many other such things you do'. He said to them,*

'All too well **you reject the commandment of God, that you may keep your tradition.** *For Moses said, Honor your father and your mother; and He who curses father or mother, let him be put to death. But you say, If a man says to his father or mother, Whatever profit you might have received from me is Corban - (that is a gift to God), then you no longer let him do anything for his father or his mother,* **making the word of God of no effect through your tradition** *which you have handed down. And many such things you do"* (Mark 7:1-13).

As is apparent from the above scriptures the religious attitude starts small, almost inconsequential, but its progression causes major damage almost making the WORD OF GOD OF NO EFFECT in the lives of those who give place to it. If this religious attitude is left unchecked in one's life it can become a demonic stronghold. From there it goes from an attitude to becoming a demon spirit or religious spirit. Rick Joyner in his book '**Overcoming the Religious Spirit**', says, *"1 A religious spirit is a demon* **which seeks to substitute religious activity for the power of the Holy Spirit** *in our lives."* I believe it is one of the greatest single obstacles in the Church, to Christianity and to bringing people to Christ, as well as keeping new converts from growing in and going on with Christ.

I have noticed in my own life over the years that I have

given place to the religious spirit. I have also noticed that it has robbed me of the anointing to serve Christ more effectively. I have also seen, through my travels all over the world preaching the 'Good News', Christian leaders bound by the religious spirit, making their ministry to the unsaved and new converts almost ineffective. They are unable to minister in love and humility, which drives many away. In the following chapters we will do a study of the religious spirit, see its slow steady progression and see how to avoid it.

CHAPTER 2

Finding Fault: the First Seed of the Religious Spirit

Mark 7:1-2, *"Then the Pharisees and some of the scribes came together to Him, having come from Jerusalem. Now when they saw some of His disciples eat bread with defiled, that is, with unwashed hands, **they found fault**."*

One of the primary ways the religious spirit manifests itself is through faultfinding. It creeps in and grows when we as Christians are critical of others. **Faultfinding can also be known as judging or the critical spirit, or pointing of the finger.** James 1:5 (NIV) says *"If any lacks wisdom, he should ask God, who gives generously to all **without finding fault,** and it will be given to him."* Our God does not find fault! Neither should we. Our God brings reproof and correction in love. This comes through the convicting power and work of the Holy Spirit.

Our ultimate example of walking in love is Jesus. And just how did He walk? Isaiah 11:3 clearly portrays it, *"His delight is in the fear of the Lord, and He shall **not judge by the sight of His eyes. Nor decide by the hearing of His ears.***" This is called discernment. We do not formulate opinions by what we see or hear; rather we look at the heart of man. When we judge people we are basically concentrating on their weaknesses and the dirt in them. We all know that when one is digging for gold, we have to dig through a lot of dirt before coming across the gold. But since we are concentrating on finding the gold, the dirt does not matter to us. Similarly, as Christians, we need to concentrate and look for the gold or good qualities in people rather than the dirt, their weaknesses.

God has put the seed of greatness and good qualities in every believer, though sometimes we have to look deeper and longer to bring them out. Proverbs 20:5 in the NIV says *"The **purposes** of a man's heart are **deep waters,** BUT **a man of understanding draws them out.***" As leaders we need to find the gold in people and bring it to the forefront. A successful ministry leader is one who has the ability or gift to find the purposes, potential and gold in people and draw it forth.

"Is this not the fast that I have chosen: To loose the bonds of wickedness, To undo the heavy burdens, To let the oppressed go free,

*And that you break every YOKE? …Then you shall call, and the Lord will answer; You shall cry, and He will say, 'Here I am.' "**If you take away the YOKE from your midst, The POINTING OF THE FINGER, and SPEAKING WICKEDNESS**"* (Isaiah 58:6 & 9). Reasons for prayer and fasting are clearly apparent in Isaiah 58:6.

a) To loose the bonds of wickedness

b) To undo heavy burdens

c) To let the oppressed go free

d) To break every yoke

Prayer and fasting changes or affects the spiritual realm, so we can affect the physical realm. As Christians we should be more in tune to the spiritual realm rather than the physical realm. One of the reasons for fasting is to **BREAK EVERY YOKE.** The yoke is bondage. It is like the yoke put on an ox for plowing. It entraps us and keeps us in bondage. When we judge we are yoked to a religious spirit. The **pointing of the finger, fault finding and judging** others is referred to as the **YOKE of bondage** in Isaiah 58:9, *"Then you shall call, and the Lord will answer; you shall cry, and He will say, Here I am. If you take away the **YOKE from your midst, the pointing of the finger, and speaking of wickedness.**"* A critical attitude may stop moves of God, destroy friendships, or cause people to mistrust each other. It can cause Christians to compete with each other, along with many other problems. It is a plague in the Body of Christ. **We need to declare war on it and drive it out.**

Hearing God's Voice

Isaiah 58:9 says that if we call upon the Lord, He will answer us and we will hear Him speak to us, but conditioned on the fact that we cease the pointing of the finger (critical spirit). Paul worded it this way in 1 Corinthians 3:1-4, *"And I, brethren, could not speak to you as to spiritual people but as to carnal, as to babes in Christ. I fed you with milk and not with solid food; for until now you were not able to receive it, and even now you are still not able; for you are still carnal. For where there are envy strife and divisions among you, are you not carnal and behaving like mere men? For when one says, 'I am of Paul,' and another, 'I am of Apollos,' are you not carnal?"* Strife and division will keep us from hearing from heaven and receiving revelation.

James 3:16(KJV) says, *"For where envying and strife is, there is confusion and every evil work."* Strife and the critical spirit actually release the destructive power of demon spirits in our midst. Holy Spirit is the one bringing revelation from heaven. But when there is strife demonic spirits are at work. It halts the flow of revelation.

Jesus talked about the power of agreement in Matthew 18:19. Then He says *"For where two or three are gathered together in My name* (in that spirit of agreement), **I am** *there* **in the midst** *of them"* (Matthew 18:20). Unity in Christ activates Christ's miracle working power and revelation knowledge from heaven.

The sum of what is being said in these verses is that revelation knowledge from God and His presence in our midst cannot be manifested amongst Christians because of the critical spirit and division. Revelation knowledge (a word from heaven) is one of the ways God helps build the Church. If there is no revelation knowledge, then the church dries up and starts to become unproductive.

Romans 10:17 says, *"So then faith comes by hearing, and hearing by the* **Word** *of God."* The Greek word for 'Word' here means spoken word. We need God to speak to us in order to accomplish His Word. When He speaks along with it comes the faith and power to accomplish what He has spoken. We can experience His divine power if we act on the word He speaks to us. All we have to do is be sensitive to hear and recognize His voice.

Jesus talked to Peter about revelation knowledge, *"He said to them 'But who do you say that I am?' Simon Peter answered and said, 'You are the Christ, the son of the living God.' Jesus answered and said to him, 'Blessed are you, Simon Bar-Jonah for flesh and blood has not revealed this to you, but my Father who is in heaven. And I also say to you that you are Peter* (Greek Petros- or small stone), *and on this rock* (Greek **Petra**- a huge rock) *I WILL BUILD MY CHURCH, AND THE GATES OF HADES SHALL NOT PREVAIL AGAINST IT"* (Matthew 16:15-18). What is this rock? Peter? No! The rock or foundation that Jesus will build His church on is REVELATION KNOWLEDGE FROM HEAVEN, which first and foremost is that Jesus is the Christ, the Son of the Living God. Nothing can stop revelation knowledge from heaven once we receive it, except allowing Satan to bring a **yoke** of bondage in our midst: **a critical spirit.** If we allow a critical spirit in, we make it difficult to hear from heaven and experience the power of God in our midst.

Numbers 12 records the incident when Aaron and Miriam judged and criticized Moses on account of his wife. Number 12:1, *"Then Miriam and Aaron spoke against Moses because of the Ethiopian woman whom he had married..."* The Lord then summons Miriam, Aaron and Moses and addresses them, Saying in verse 8 *"...Why then were you not afraid to speak against My servant Moses? So the anger of the Lord was aroused against them, and He departed."* As a result of their grumbling, Miriam was struck with leprosy and had to stay outside the camp for an entire week. The people did not journey for that period of time, till Miriam was restored. Moses had to intercede on Miriam's behalf, for the Lord's anger to be averted.

When a critical spirit enters in we become FRUIT INSPECTORS rather than FRUIT PRODUCERS. This problem smothers many churches. It restricts growth. People operating in this mode often hop from church to church looking for the perfect church. The only problem is they will never find a perfect church. It is hard to grow spiritually without being firmly planted in a good local church.

Health Problems: Fruit of a Critical Spirit

Another problem brought into our lives by a critical spirit are health afflictions. A critical spirit can keep our health from springing forth speedily (see Isaiah 58:8). A critical spirit can bring in bitterness, anger, offense, impatience and health problems like cancer, arthritis and others. The medical profession has proven being bitter, angry, offensive, impatient, resentful, or unforgiving can actually change a person's body chemistry and make them more prone to illness.

Do not get me wrong. Not everyone who has health problems, cancer or arthritis necessarily has a critical spirit or is struggling with anger. For some that is the case. In these cases a critical spirit needs to be dealt with, if we want a permanent healing and/or deliverance.

37

Over the years while ministering in healing services and open air campaigns I have noticed that where the churches and/or leaders are walking in offense, and are critical it hinders God from moving powerfully in their midst. A good example of this is found in Mark 6:1-6. In verse 3 it talks about how the people from Jesus' hometown of Nazareth were critical and offended by Jesus. Mark 6:5-6 says *"Now He **could do no mighty work there,** except that He laid His hands on a few sick people and healed them. And HE MARVELED BECAUSE OF THEIR UNBELIEF..."* Here you can see how a critical spirit, offense and unbelief work hand in hand. Jesus could have set them free but their being offended with Him prevented them from receiving their miracle.

Luke 5:17-26 records a similar situation. Verse 17 *"And the **Power of the Lord was present to heal them."** If you read this story only one person walked away with a miracle. Yet God's power was present to heal many people not just one person. Verse 21 shows us why. It is because the religious leaders, bound by a religious spirit were reasoning in their minds, critical and offended with Jesus.

We need to stop being critical and offended with leaders and other believers God has put in our life. It will stop the power of the Lord from flowing to you and through you. The critical spirit, offense and unbelief clog the pipeline so God's power cannot flow to others. Psalm 119:165 (KJV) says *Great peace have they* that love thy law: and *nothing shall offend them.* Colossians 3:3 says *For you died, and your life is hidden with Christ in God.* Think about it! How can a dead man get offended?

I have noticed in services where the people are dealing with the critical spirit and offense or are walking free from these spirits that God moves powerfully. Dealing with the critical spirit, offense along with prayer and sometimes fasting sets the spiritual atmosphere for God to move powerfully. In these kinds of services most walk away with their miracles from Jesus. We know pastors who can testify of this.

Critical Spirit: Perversion of Godly Discernment

Many Christians feel it is alright to judge people. 1 Corinthians 2:15 says, *"But he who is spiritual judges all **things**, yet he himself is rightly judged by no one."* Matthew 7:1 says, *"Judge not lest you be judged."* This sounds like a contradiction. I Corinthians 2:15 in the amplified explains it clearly *"But the spiritual man tries all **things** [that is,] he examines, investigates, inquires into, questions, and discerns all things."* Notice this verse says he *"**judges all things,**"* **not people.**

There is a major difference between using discernment

verses judging someone. Isaiah 11:3 defines true spirituality and discernment. This is a prophecy about the Messiah: Jesus who was to come. It says, *"... He shall not judge by the sight of His eyes, nor decide by the hearing of His ears."* True spirituality and discernment is not judging and condemning one another. It is looking beyond the external circumstances and seeing a person's heart as God sees him or her.

When we judge and condemn others we are setting ourselves up for a fall from grace. Rick Joyner states in an article in the Morning Star Journal entitled Prophetic Character, *"[2]When we criticize another Christian or church, we are declaring that the Lord's own workmanship does not meet our standards."* We are also saying we are better than that person. The Pharisees of Jesus day had this problem and they missed out on the Author of life itself, Jesus.

Critical Spirit – vs. - Discernment

Critical Spirit	Discernment
a) Will cause you to burn out and dry up.	A) Operates in God's love and anointing. No burn out or drying up.
b) Operates in pride - Example, Pharisees of Jesus' day.	B) Operates in humility - Example, Jesus Christ.
c) Modern day heresy hunter. Feeding frenzy (like sharks).	C) Encourages people in their gifts. Sees the gold in people. Love is how the world sees we are His disciples.
d) Everybody but me mentality, "I wish another person were here to hear this one. He really needs this."	D) Searches heart motives on a frequent basis. Open to correction and necessary ministry.
e) Religious Spirit, no relationship with God. Too busy with religious activity.	E) Relationship with God. Has time for intimacy with God.
f) Guilty no matter what! Shoots our wounded! No bearing of burdens.	F) Innocent until proven guilty! If guilty, forgives bearing of burdens.
g) Gossips about…	G) Intercedes for…

Critical people usually miss out on revival. Individuals operating in godly discernment, walking daily with Jesus, are kept from falling into error. They are able to discern what is of God and what is not. They are poised and ready for a move of God.

The critical spirit has caused many to become "heresy hunters" a realm of ministry that is totally contrary to God's heart and nature. Many Christians have naively embraced these ministries. A man known years ago for being an expert on exposing cults also began to be publicly critical and cut down other Christian men and women of God with whom he disagreed. A short time later he died of cancer. Many have followed in his footsteps, blasting other members of the body of Christ. Some have fallen into legal and moral problems as they continue to operate in a critical spirit. You reap what you sow when you begin to judge Christ's workmanship.

Rick Joyner states in his book, **The Surpassing Greatness of His Power,** *"[3]Numerous leaders have spent their lives serving faithfully and well, only to end up as vessels for the accuser, who makes them a stumbling block for the next move."* He prophesied this, January of 1989 in an article entitled **An Onslaught Against the Church,** *"[4]The accuser of the brethren has been released with unprecedented rage. Satan's highest goal is to get* *brethren accusing and dividing against another."*

How to Walk Free from a Critical Spirit

The critical spirit and offense are one of the strongest manifestations of arrogance and pride. We will deal with that subject in the next chapter. There have been times in my life and ministry when a critical spirit kept me bound. It kept the anointing from flowing freely through me. There are some keys I have used in order to walk free of the critical spirit. First we have to recognize this critical spirit and repent of being critical. Secondly Amos 3:3 says, *"Can two walk together unless they are agreed?"* The answer is no. We have to fall out of agreement with this spirit. Thirdly Romans 12:21, *"Do not be overcome by evil, but overcome evil with good."* Start by doing the opposite, renewing your mind to God's word (see Romans 12:2), and then working out that which is contrary to being critical and judgmental (refer to earlier list).

The fourth key is to separate ourselves from people (including Christians) who are always critical. I find that when I am in the company of people who are critical on a continual basis then I become critical. *"EVIL COMPANY CORRUPTS GOOD HABITS"* (1 Corinthians 15:33). Paul states in Romans 16:17 *"Now I urge you, brethren, note **those who cause division and offense,** contrary to the doctrine which you learned, and*

AVOID THEM." Division and offense were contrary to Paul's doctrine! One of Paul's doctrines was keeping the unity of the spirit in the bond of peace and walking in love, which believes the best of each person (see 1 Corinthians 13:7 amplified).

In order for some people to break free from a critical spirit they need to break the curse that comes with being judgmental. In some cases we need to break generational curses that have stopped the blessings of God because of the "pointing finger" that has been passed from generation to generation.

Another way to keep from being critical is to take a good look at oneself. The older I get I see how I am unable to judge others when I do that. We need to realize that we are destined to work with each other despite our problems and differences. So we better get on with it. We need to fit in where we belong and start using the gifts God has given us to do our part in the Body of Christ.

A United Body

Proverbs 6:16-19 says *these six things the Lord hates, yes seven are an abomination to Him.* (#1) - *is **a proud look*** and he finishes with (#7) - *one **who sows discord among the brethren.*** Despite going through difficulties initially for taking this stand against judging, I have learned to stay clear of and disassociate myself from people who are constantly critical and judgmental. Why?

44

Because God hates arrogance. God calls gossip, division and a critical spirit an abomination to Him. That's pretty strong! God has blessed us in so many ways for taking this stand years ago.

Working together and fellowshipping with other brothers and sisters in Christ should be a high priority on our list. In Genesis 11:6 we find a very profound statement made by God Himself: *"And the Lord said, 'INDEED THE PEOPLE ARE ONE and they all have one language, and this is what they begin to do; NOW NOTHING THAT THEY PURPOSE TO DO WILL BE WITHHELD FROM THEM.'* What is sad here is that they purposed to do evil and God had to confuse their language (vs. 7).

Imagine if we, the Body of Christ, became so unified in our talk and purpose. Nothing would be withheld from us. This was Jesus' prayer in John 17:21 *"that they ALL MAY BE ONE, as You, Father, are in me, and I in You; that they may be one in us, that the WORLD MAY BELIEVE THAT YOU SENT ME."* God's heart cry is for His Body, the Church, to be one.

One Christian leader I have had great admiration for over the years is Apostle George Hill, of the Victory Churches International organization. He has a saying that has stuck in my heart for years: ***"united action produces effectiveness."*** This saying is true and it is in line with God's heart.

There are cities throughout this world that have had this vision for unity and united action and as a result many thousands have come to Christ in these cities. Cali, Columbia was transformed by the power of churches united for one purpose, to lift up Jesus (see John 12:32).

We the, Body of Christ are Jesus' expression of Himself to this lost and dying world. *"And He put all things under His feet, and gave Him to be the head over all things to the CHURCH, which is HIS BODY, THE FULNESS OF HIM who fills all in all"*(Ephesians 1:22-23). The Church is the FULNESS OF CHRIST ON THE EARTH. Only when we become one united body will the world **fully see Christ.**

"Behold, how good and how pleasant it is for brethren to dwell together IN UNITY! It is like the PRECIOUS OIL upon the head,…for there the Lord COMMANDED A BLESSING, life forevermore" (Psalm 133:1-3). God's heart is for the entire Body of Christ, the Church, to work together in unity. In that kind of environment there is a tremendous anointing. Verse 2 refers to unity as oil. Oil also symbolizes the anointing. The Holy Spirit, the one who anoints us, works mightily in an atmosphere of unity.

Verse 3 tells us God COMMANDS BLESSINGS to flow when His Body, the Church, operates in unity. We have experienced an increase of blessings and favor since this attitude became our passion. A religious spirit concentrates only on uniting with those who will believe exactly as we do or are in the same organization. That is the same demonic spirit that operates in political circles to keep everyone politically correct, as the nation spirals downward. I write more in-depth about this in Chapter 14. I do not believe that is the stand Jesus would take. The early Church was in one accord most of the time and learned to disagree agreeably. You can see how powerfully God moved in the early Church because of their unity. To win the lost we should **unite around the simple fact that Jesus Christ is Lord.**

Judging causes us to be blind to our own problems

The critical spirit is completely contrary to the nature of God. Jesus said, *"JUDGE NOT, that you be not judged. For with what judgment you judge, you will be judged; and with the measure you use, it will be measured back to you. And why do you look at the speck in your brother's eye, but do not consider the plank in your own eye"* (Matthew 7:1-3)? Judging will BLIND us to our own problems. An "anyone else but me can do wrong" mentality will diminish our effectiveness for God's glory. It brings in an arrogant attitude that God says He will resist (see James 4:6). It also drives away those we need to reach for Christ.

Paul said, *"Therefore you have no excuse or defense or justification, O man, whoever you are who judges and condemns another. For in posing as a judge and passing sentence on another* **you CONDEMN yourself,** *because you who judge are habitually practicing the very same things* [that you denounce]" (Romans 2:1 amplified). When we judge others we condemn ourselves. Judging is like a mirror. We tend to become what we behold and meditate upon. Proverbs 23:7 says, *"For as a man thinks in his heart so is he."* If we meditate or picture something on a regular basis we will become that very thing. When we criticize and condemn others it operates like a mirror. We become what we behold. If we judge others, we are criticizing God's workmanship. We are no better, and Satan has won. I find praising God and seeing the good in people a lot better than operating in criticism.

If we have faults with one another, the scriptural way to deal with it is found in Matthew 18:15, *"Moreover if your brother* **sins against you,** (Greek -misses the mark, trespasses) *go and tell him his fault BETWEEN YOU AND HIM ALONE.* (Here is the heart of God) *If he hears you, YOU HAVE GAINED YOUR BROTHER."* How many ministers or Christians operate by this code?

Maintaining a Proper Heart Attitude

God's heart is for unity despite our doctrinal differences. He's not asking us to compromise our beliefs. Which is more important heart attitude or doctrine and theology? God's heart is not as much for our doctrinal beliefs as it is for our heart's attitude. Don't get me wrong our doctrines and beliefs are important **but to God our heart attitude is of primary importance.** Jesus said in Matthew 5:8 *Blessed are the pure in heart, For they shall see God.* Notice Jesus did not say those who have the best doctrine or theology will see God. He said those who have a heart that is pure will see Him in action. *For the eyes of the Lord run to and fro throughout the whole earth, to shew himself strong in the behalf of them whose heart is perfect toward him.*(2 Chronicles 16:9 KJV).

The Pharisees of Jesus' day would put us to shame with the way they studied the word of God and knew it. The problem was that their pride and critical spirit caused them to pervert scripture and miss out on what it is all about: Jesus the Christ. They had an evil heart. Let us not become like a modern Pharisee. We stagnate when our hearts become unteachable, critical, prideful and controlling.

The larger or more successful we become in ministry the more susceptible we are to the danger of pride and a critical spirit creeping in. Our success can be our downfall if we do not guard our heart.

Many times we expect others whose ministries are not as large or successful as ours to be serving the Lord in the same capacity as we are. Every person is different. Everything we have has only come by the grace of God. *Not that we are sufficient of ourselves to think any thing as of ourselves; but our sufficiency is of God* (2 Corinthians 3:5).

There is a difference between **challenging others and having a critical spirit.** Know where to draw the line. A critical spirit only sees the negative and never helps someone rise above his/her failures or shortcomings. Being critical of other's shortcomings can set one up for a fall. To honest with you, I have seen this happen way too often in the Body Christ.

A critical spirit destroys close friendships. It brings misconceptions of someone who has a pure heart and pure motives for God. Many who have been wounded in churches (maybe by a critical spirit) become critical, judgmental, and defensive if they do not guard their hearts. I have learned that relationships can terminate even if your heart has been right. Continue to maintain a good heart. Do not become critical or defensive, and then God can move you on to bigger and better opportunities for His glory. He has done this for us and it has turned out so much better than we ever imagined. It has been amazing when people judged our motives wrongly and doors closed as a result, we moved on and kept our hearts right. As a result it worked out even better in the long run because bigger and better opportunities arose. It has helped us to greatly expand and produce more lasting fruit than if we would have remained in those other circles, where the doors closed.

It is when we go through hard times that our heart is tested. These are also the crucial times when what is really inside us surfaces. Do not give in to a critical spirit at those times. *"Keep your heart with all diligence, For out of it spring the issues of life"*(Proverbs 4:23). Choose to walk in love, believing the best of others, blessing others and keeping your heart right. God does have better things in store. Study Isaiah 58 and see the benefits of abstaining from the "pointing finger," from a critical spirit. Staying free from a critical spirit will put you over in life and ministry quicker, with God's blessings overtaking you.

CHAPTER 3

Pride & False Humility

"For the Pharisees and all the Jews do not eat unless they wash their hands in a special way, holding the traditions of the elders"(Mark 7:3).

Many of the religious leaders during the days of Jesus strictly adhered to the Law of Moses. It became an issue of spiritual pride. Unfortunately, they also added other rules and regulations to the Law, making abiding by them virtually impossible. Many of these religious leaders were elitist, prideful and boastful. They made the common man feel guilty if they were unable to keep the law and live up to their rules. Many of these religious leaders were arrogant and passionate in their beliefs in the way they came across to others. Their passion was a good example of misplaced passion.

Their passion made them self-righteous snobs in the way they presented their beliefs and came across to the common person of their day.

As a young minister I was passionate about souls and certain teachings. When others did not act and believe as I did my passion turned to pride, offense and a critical spirit. As I look back at those days I remember the anointing I had to win people to Christ one on one. When I allowed myself to become critical and offended I began to dry up spiritually in my life. Do not allow your passion to turn into offense and a critical spirit. Guard your heart. A critical spirit will quench the anointing of God in your life.

In the previous chapter we covered judging and the critical spirit as one the gateways in opening up to a religious spirit. One the greatest manifestations of arrogance is the critical spirit and judging. Who are we to judge Christ's workmanship? It is like telling God I do not like the way you made that person. We call it for what it is. That is arrogance, elitism and pride!

The religious spirit also manifests itself in pride and self-righteousness. Pride and self-exaltation caused Satan to fall and to be thrown out of heaven (see Isaiah 14:12-14). Proverbs 6:16-19 says *"These six things the Lord hates, Yes seven are an abomination to Him: A proud look, a lying tongue...he who sows discord among brethren."*

The Anointing can Transform Lives

Division and discord come as a result of the pride of man. As Christians we are all playing on the same team. We should not be in competition with each other; rather each should do his or her part, working together to further the kingdom of God. Our desire should be to see those we train to excel and supersede us. When I first wrote about this subject in 2000 I sensed a greater anointing coming upon myself in the area of divine healing and miracles. The reason is not because I am anyone special, but partially a direct result of what the Lord spoke to me February of 2000; and I put it into practice. He told me that the more I trained and released other people in the area of healing and miracles, the greater the anointing would be upon my life. My strong desire is to see the ministry of those whom I train or disciple to surpass my own ministry. To me that is good fruit that goes right into eternity.

At the time the Lord laid these things on my heart we were in Nicaragua. I had a friend, Matt, traveling with me. Matt had a desire for some time to preach in evangelistic campaigns, but never had the opportunity. We were conducting an open-air campaign in the rural village of Dulce Nombre. On the third night of a four-day campaign I had Matt share for a few minutes to encourage the crowd. He struggled trying to share, not sensing much of an anointing.

The next morning I talked to him about his difficulty in sharing. I encouraged and briefed him in the proper method of ministering during a campaign. This was the final day of the campaign. I once again asked him to share that night. I told him to minister as long as he felt led and sensed the anointing. If he were unable to continue, I would take over and complete ministering to the people.

That night I could sense some people were uncomfortable with him sharing again, since he had such a difficult time the previous night. As he started preaching the anointing of God came on Matt and he sounded like a seasoned preacher. I did not get the opportunity to preach that night. Forty-five minutes later he gave the altar call for salvation. Many came forward. Together we prayed a mass prayer for healing. More people were saved and healed that night than the previous three nights together.

Within one year Matt had many other invitations to preach in Nicaragua, El Salvador and the USA. One year later he conducted an open-air campaign and personal evangelism training school in Nicaragua. God used him powerfully as many came to Christ and many miracles occurred. The anointing of

God can transform a believer in an instant, as in Matt's case. We need to believe and see the potential in other Christians as we mentioned before when talking about digging for gold and Proverbs 20:5 (NIV) in the previous chapter.

In God's kingdom, the way up is the way down. We should be willing to fit into whatever mold God wants us to be in and be willing to serve. *"Therefore humble yourselves under the mighty hand of God, that He may exalt you in due time"*(1 Peter 5:6). God's desire is to lift us up and take us beyond where we have been. In order to do this we need to be humble and obedient. **Pride always will focus on one small part of the puzzle but HUMILITY will affect the big picture.**

James 4:6 says *"But He gives more grace. Therefore He says: God resists the proud, but gives **grace to the humble.**"* How do we fulfill our ministry? Only by the grace of God! Every gift we have is because of His grace. The more we humble ourselves, the more His grace abounds upon us to fulfill the task at hand.

The leaders in Jesus' day operated in a false humility that was nothing more than a facade. They directed the focus of the people on all the sacrifices they made, which was false humility, rooted in pride and arrogance. The religious spirit will try to divert the attention to **one's personal cross and try to glorify it,** rather than the **Cross of Christ.** All this is done in sublime ways portraying what one has done for Jesus, the persecution, hardships and sacrifices encountered for Him - all centered on the I and self. This is a clear contradiction of what Paul says in Galatians 6:14 *"But God forbid that I should boast except in the Cross of the our Lord Jesus Christ."* Jesus said in Matthew 6:1-6 that if we do it before men - our praying and giving then we have our reward; that is, men would exalt and glorify us but not God.

We need to seek the favor and honor of God above all else. The attention always needs to be on Jesus. Jesus told the Pharisees, *"**you are of your father the devil...**"*(John 8:44). The devil was a liar and prideful. Pride causes exaggeration and lying. We need to be people of integrity. Pride will cause us to be insecure in whom God made us to be, boasting in and exaggerating our accomplishments. We do not have to be man pleasers. We need to live our lives for the audience of One. Our security needs to be in God. We do not have to strive to make ourselves look good to man.

True promotion comes from God not man. Psalm 75:6-7 says *For exaltation comes neither from the east Nor from the west nor from the south. But God is the Judge: He puts down one, And exalts another.* Despite the circumstances you can be put over by God if you understand how promotion in His kingdom works.

The way up is down low.

Do you desire to know whom He exalts and whom He puts down? Psalm 138:6 tells us *Though the LORD is on high, Yet He regards the lowly; But the proud He knows from afar.* James 4:6, 8, 10 says *But He gives more grace. Therefore He says: " God resists the proud, But gives grace to the humble." Draw near to God and He will draw near to you. Humble yourselves in the sight of the Lord, and He will lift you up* (James 4:6, 8, &10). We need to draw near to our God in order to tap into His power, grace and blessing. How do you draw near to Him? Remain humble and He will promote you. The truly humble will carry His nature and anointing to a hurting world.

Competition in the Body of Christ

"Do nothing out of selfish ambition (KJV- strife) or vain conceit, but in **humility consider others** *better than yourselves. Each of you should look not only to your own interests, but also to the interests of others. Your attitude* **should be the same as that of Christ Jesus:** *Who, being in very nature God, did not consider equality with God something to be grasped,* **but made Himself nothing,** *taking the very* **nature of a servant,** *being made in human likeness. And being found in appearance as a man,* **He humbled Himself** *and became obedient to death- even death on a cross! Therefore God* **exalted Him to the highest place** *and gave Him the name that*

is above every name, that at the name of Jesus every knee should bow, in heaven and on earth and under the earth, and every tongue confess that Jesus Christ is Lord, to the glory of God the Father" (Philippians 2:3-11 NIV).

In order to become the unified army that God is looking for, to reap the end time harvest, the Body of Christ needs to walk in a spirit of humility. Many things are being done in the Body of Christ out of selfish ambition, strife and competition rather than for the simple love of Christ and for souls. We should strive to have the mind of Christ. It is an attitude of humility, an attitude that cares for the interests of others. Our goals should not be to see how we can out do other Christians, churches or ministries, but to reach the lost.

Proverbs 13:10 says *"Only **by pride comes contention:** but with the well advised is wisdom."* Much of Christianity today has seen churches and ministries in strife, contention and competition with each other. Instead of fighting the real enemy (Satan and demons) for souls, we are fighting each other. Often our actions are **motivated by what** makes us, our church or ministry **look good** rather than caring about the interests of others. We come across as arrogant, elitist and prideful to the unsaved, just as the Pharisees and Sadducees of Jesus' day. I have been guilty of the same.

It is sad when we begin to think that God cannot do anything of significance unless it is through us, our organization, denomination or our ministry. Pride causes many to slow down or fall by the wayside with jealousy whenever God uses someone else more powerfully than us. Whatever gifts and talents we have as individuals or in a church organization comes only by God's grace. Remember, apart from Him we can do nothing (see John 15:5). This should cause us to walk in humility.

*"Therefore **judge nothing before the time,** until the Lord come, who both will bring **to light the hidden things of darkness, and will make manifest the counsel of the hearts:** and then shall every man have praise of God. And these things, brethren, I have in a figure transfers to myself and to Apollos for your sakes; that you might learn in us not to think of men above that which is written that **no one of you be puffed for one against another.** For who makes you to differ from another? And what do you have that you did not receive? Now if you did receive it, why do you glory, as if you had not received it"*(1 Corinthians 4:5-7)?

It says not to judge others. Judging is the result of pride. It says in the Scripture not to glory in our gift, because whatever most dominant good we have is God given. In my chapter on Humility and the Glory I will discuss indepth the glory of man shutting down the Glory of God. Many times we lift up one ministry against another as though we are in competition with each other. Alas! We are missing the entire point. It is not about our church, our ministry or us. It is all about Jesus and souls! Instead of competing with each other we should be doing our best to help fill other churches, as well as our own, with new believers. That is God's heartbeat, souls.

Many years ago I was in Virginia, Minnesota teaching on personal evangelism in a small church. I shared with this church God's heart for the lost. I taught on not lifting up your church more than lifting up Jesus Christ when sharing with the lost. Jesus said in John 12:32 *"And I, **if I am lifted up** from the earth, **will draw all peoples to Myself.**"*

The pastor and the congregation went out regularly sharing Christ with the lost after the training. They led many people to Christ and there was great excitement in the church. Their approach was to simply lift up Christ. It did not matter to them what church these people became a part of. It became all about winning lost souls for this church. As a result many other churches were filled with the people they led to Christ. One pastor called this pastor and thanked him for winning people to Christ who were now attending his church. As a result of the heart attitude of this small church God quickly expanded them as well. This is what Philippians 2:4 is talking about.

When we humble ourselves, God increases the grace upon us to accomplish the task at hand. The task at hand is to bring in the harvest of souls Jesus died for as opposed to building our own little kingdom. Let us get back to the task at hand.

Many of us have humble beginnings. It is when God begins to exalt us and gives us victories that we need to be on the guard against arrogance. Success can make one more susceptible to arrogance and the fall. It sneaks up most of the time right after a great victory. Even though a person may start off walking in humility, it is no guarantee that he will continue the same way. The greater our accomplishments the greater the danger of becoming full of pride. We must guard our hearts from pride and arrogance. Humility will cause God to continue to exalt us and increase the grace for the call He has placed on our life. It will help us to stand strong and go much farther.

When we come to a place where **we esteem others better than ourselves** that is when we as the Body of Christ **will cause others to go even further in Christ.** Jesus, the greater, laid down His life for the lesser, us. How many of us think this way; to cause others to become and look better than ourselves.

How to Stay Standing

1 Corinthians 10:12 says *"Wherefore let him that thinks he stands take heed lest he fall."* Many times we may look at

others judging and criticizing them for shortcomings thinking that we would never do the same. This attitude sets us up for a fall. Galatians 6:1 tells us to **Restore** (Greek – **bring back to usefulness**) people, *"... in a spirit of gentleness* (meekness-KJV), *considering yourself lest you also be tempted."*

Many Christians allow themselves to walk in pride because of insecurity or the desire to be in control. Insecurity and shame are byproducts of arrogance. *When pride comes* [boiling up with an arrogant attitude of self-importance], *then come dishonor and shame* (Proverbs 11:2 Amp). Some Christians are actually happy when another brother, sister or minister falls or fails as they think it may make them look better. Our pride can drive us to a place where we feel vindictive and vengeful. We do not like people because of insecurities, competition or because we want people to recognize us. This is not the attitude of Christ.

Notice the attitude humility takes on even in the midst of being attacked, as recorded in Numbers 12, when Miriam and Aaron spoke against Moses. *Now the man Moses was very* **meek above all the men which were upon the face of the earth** (Numbers 12:3). Miriam was struck with leprosy for coming against Moses (vs10). Aaron cried for mercy (vs11-12).

What was this meek man Moses' response? Vengeance? Hatred? No! It was **compassion**. Verse 13, *"Moses cried unto the*

Lord, saying, heal her now, O God, I beseech thee." How many of us Christian would take on a similar attitude of blessing someone who has caused us great pain? God answered Moses' cry. One week later she was free of leprosy.

When we allow anger, impatience, spite and vengeance to creep in we are giving place to pride. Let God deal with that person. Pray for God's mercy on that person. That is walking in true humility. Jesus prayed on the cross, *"Father forgive them for they know not what they do"* (Luke 23:34).

Servant of all

*"But Jesus called them to Himself and said, 'you know that the rulers of the **Gentiles lord it over them,** and those who are great exercise authority over them. Yet it shall **not be so among you;** but whoever desires to **become great** among you, **let him be your servant.** And whoever desires to be first among you, let him be your slave- just as the Son of Man did not come to be served, **but to serve, and to give His life a ransom for many"** (Matthew 20:25-28).

Jesus, our ultimate example of a leader and whose authority we are under, came with humility to serve those He came in contact with. It should be our highest desire to follow in His footsteps. To follow Him is to be humble and serve others out of a pure heart with no ulterior motives.

Once while ministering in India I was training pastors, leaders and their church members on this principle. I let them know this was God's heart for India. When I finished I was pulled aside by several of the leading pastors to discuss these things. I thought that maybe God had really challenged them by this teaching. Instead they questioned my teaching. They rebuked me saying that I needed to teach the church members to serve them rather than they serving. They were greatly offended by my teaching on servanthood. Even though we had worked together for some time with great fruit being reaped, since that day they no longer wanted to work with our ministry. Would that be the position Jesus would have taken? That very attitude among many leaders in India is why many unsaved are turned off to Christianity and slipping into eternity without Christ.

Years ago I was teaching in Kathmandu, Nepal at the Sowers Ministry Missions Training Center. I was greatly impressed by the students and the staff. During one of the classes the director, Sandy Anderson, and his staff came in the classroom with buckets of water, soap and towels. He shared from John 13:12-17 which is as follows, *"So when He had washed their feet, taken His garments, and sat down again, He said to them, "Do you know what I have done to you? You call me Teacher and Lord, and you say well, for so I am. If I then your Lord and Teacher have* *washed your feet, you ought to wash one another's feet. For I have given you an example, that you should do as I have done to you. Most assuredly, I say to you, a servant is not greater than his master; nor is he who is sent greater than he who sent him. **If you know these things, blessed are you if you do them.**"*

Sandy Anderson shared God's heart to serve the lost and Christians in Nepal. Then he, his staff and those with me joined in and washed the students feet. The presence of God filled that classroom. I did not see a student with a dry eye in that room.

Humility is...

Humility will cause us to lift up Jesus more than self, a church or a ministry. **Humility** will drive us to make disciples for Jesus rather than for man. **Humility** will compel us to decrease and Christ to increase (see John 3:30). **Humility** will serve rather than be served or control others (see John 13:1-17). **Humility** will teach us to learn from and work with the entire body of Christ. **Humility** will make us transparent rather than untouchable. **Humility** will stir us to raise up others to be much more effective in ministry than ourselves and rejoice when they surpass us (see Ephesians 4:11-12). **Humility** makes us secure in who God made us to be. **Humility** will not do things for recognition but for the sake of the gospel. **Humility** does not act out of competition or jockey for position, but looks for a need and meets it.

Humility will reveal to the world the One they need most: JESUS CHRIST. **Humility** will prepare us to be the end time warriors Christ has called us to be with great courage and will cause the glory of God to manifest in our lives so the world can see Jesus. **Humility** is what will seat us on the thrones next to Jesus for eternity (see Mark 10:35-45). Mark10:40 shows us the thrones are for those who with a **humble** heart, in this life, are willing to serve the least of these (see also Matthew 25:31-46). Finally, **humility is the nature of Christ in you!**

In Chapter 6 we will deal with humility and the glory much more indepth. I will cover how humility is needed to bring the glory of God to earth and needed for a lasting move of God. We share also how the glory of man or arrogance has many times shut down the move of God over a region. I will also share some powerful testimonies of the glory of God manifesting on earth in recent days.

CHAPTER 4

Holding on to Manmade Traditions

*"When they come from the marketplace, they do not eat unless they wash. And there are many things, which they have received and hold, like the washing of cups, pitchers, copper vessels and couches. Then the Pharisees and scribes asked Him, Why do your disciples not walk according to the **traditions of the elders,** but eat bread with unwashed hands"*(Mark 7:4-5).

As the religious spirit progresses, traditions and adhering to them become more important than anything else, including God's word and work. It was men, bound by religious traditions who strangled William Tyndale to death on October 6, 1536, because he dared to translate the Bible into English.

In the early 1500s the only legal Bible was in the Latin

language. Since the common people could not understand it, they could not read the Word of God for themselves and had to rely on what others told them. In fact it was illegal to own an English Bible or even memorize Scripture in English. A Doctor of Divinity in England came severely against Tyndale for translating the Bible into English. In the argument between the two Tyndale quoted Scripture while the Doctor quoted man-made traditions and church rules. Finally the Doctor of Divinity shouted, *"It would be better to be without God's law than without the Pope's."* Tyndale had to go into hiding, but was ultimately caught and martyred for the sake of Jesus by the clergy of England, who were influenced by this same religious spirit that operated in Jesus' day.

The religious spirit also tries to clone people into a religious mode. We see this leaking into the political realm today, where ungodly politicians try to control the masses by touting 'politically correct rhetoric' to fulfill their selfish agendas. God has made everyone unique and different. If I expected everyone to be like me, operate and minister like me; and then I get critical and judgmental if they do not, then I am wrong and being controlled by the religious spirit. A dominating critical spirit causes us to expect all things to be done our way; and if not we have no use for the people concerned. We tell them *"it is my way or the highway."* This attitude is a stench to the nostrils of God, yet it's common in the Body of Christ. We need to have grace towards all and permit them to function in the gift and call that God has upon their life, maintaining proper checks and balances, without being controlling.

Offering only Lip Service to God

*"He answered and said to them, well did Isaiah prophesy of you hypocrites, as it is written: "This people **honors Me with their lips,** But their **heart is far from Me.** And in vain they worship Me, **Teaching as doctrines the commandments of men"***(Mark 7:6 -7).

Isaiah prophesied that these people would only offer lip service to God, and their hearts would be far from God. The religious spirit leads us down the empty and dangerous path of lip service only to the Most High God. Externally, we appear to be committed to the Lord; speaking our Christianese and doing all the right things, though internally we are empty and cold towards the Lord. Most of the religions of today are this way, unfortunately including Christianity to some extent.

The progression of the religious spirit is so apparent as we meditate on Mark 7:7 where it says, *"and in vain they worship Me, **teaching as doctrines the commandments of men."*** If the lip service only to God is not dealt with then the next down hill step is vain or useless worship of and to Him. What is even worse than that is the teaching of the commandments of men. **What happened to the commandments of God?**

Commands of Men

In 1555 John Denley was burned at the stake because he believed in the commands of God. The Church of England did not like that. John Denley believed that the Church was built upon the apostles and prophets with Christ as its Chief Cornerstone. Many of the teachings of the Church of England were not according to the Bible. They were teaching the commands of men.

In 1527 Patrick Hamilton was also burned at the stake in Scotland because he believed that the Bible, not the edicts of the established church (commands of men), held the true foundation of the Christian faith and the relationship of each person to God. He boldly preached these truths and was arrested for disturbing the established church. When he refused to refrain from preaching and to change his beliefs, he was sentenced to death. People under the influence of a religious spirit were so insensitive to the truth, that they thought nothing of putting men and women to death simply because they dared to pursue the truth and an intimate relationship with their Maker.

We should not get side-tracked from Biblical truths to

pursue the commands of men that go against God's word and are heavy burdens and hard to keep. In Matthew 11:28 Jesus says, *"Come to Me, all you who labor and are* **heavy laden,** (Greek-**overburdened with ceremony**) *and I will give you* **rest."** The religious leaders hated Jesus, because He promised the people freedom from religious burdens. He continues in Matthew 11:29-30, *"Take My yoke upon you and learn from Me, for I am gentle and lowly in heart, and you will find rest for your souls. For My yoke is easy and My burden is light."* The reason His task and burden is easy is because we do it in His strength once we come to a place of intimacy and humility with Him.

In the Fall of 1988, the Lord addressed me saying, **"Mark, I have called you to an intimate relationship with me and out of that intimacy I want all your works to be birthed, nothing apart from it."** In other words, He was saying that my works were to be birthed through prayer and communion with Him, rather than any religious duty. As I have obeyed Him in the years since, this ministry has seen a greater manifestation of the power and compassion of God and produced much more and lasting fruit.

Many Christians are driven and feel overloaded. I used to feel this way, until Jesus spoke to me and set me free. One of the primary reasons for being driven is the lack of an intimate relationship with Jesus and not learning to be meek, lowly or humble like Him. When we become meek and humble it brings rest. How? It frees us from the need of proving ourselves to others. We do not have to do things any more to save face and please man. We do everything to please God and for the sake of the cross. We do things for the **audience of ONE,** His audience only!

In John 5:44, Jesus puts it this way, *"How can you believe, which receive* **honor** *one of another, and seek not the honor that* ***comes from God only.***" So many today spend much time promoting self and their accomplishments. From there it leads to exaggeration (better known as lying or hype). They do this because their desire is to win man's favor.

Rick Joyner's book **"The Final Quest"** states, *"⁵Everything that you do to exalt yourself will one day bring the most terrible humiliation."* Proverbs 16:18 says Pride goes before destruction, a haughty spirit before a fall. How many have fallen because they were obsessed with promoting self. Satan fell for this reason (see Isaiah 14:12-15 and Ezekiel 28:12-17). Then he came down to earth and made Adam and Eve fall because of pride. Also in **The Final Quest,** *"⁶the more influence that you gain by your own self promotion, the more you must strive to retain your influence, and the more dark and cruel your life will become."* Without having intimacy with God and being infused with Christlike humility many are driven into a place of self-promotion, pride and dead religious works.

There have been leaders who with a humble heart served God, but then to look good and successful started exaggerating (lying) to promote what they were doing. Soon they no longer recognized the lies and deception that came in, or chose to ignore it, to save face and look good to man. How sad! Along with this came stagnation and Holy Spirit was grieved and quenched. Eventually many of them fell from grace!

It is time that we the Body of Christ, for the sake of the gospel, cease being concerned with saving face and start walking in humility and love towards all. If these ingredients are not intact, the harvest will rot while we look to save face. One day we will have to give an account to Jesus as to why we let the harvest fields of the world rot, while trying to save face. In recent years I have seen people of God looking and seeking their own glory more than the glory of God. As result they are given to hype, selfish ambition, the glory of man, exaggeration, deception and much more. They pursue the gifts, power, recognition, etc more than they pursue a living relationship with their Creator, Jesus Christ. What does it accomplish in the long run. The glory of God will lift and find another place to fall where people with a humble heart will be used to manifest His glory on this earth.

The actions of one bound by the religious spirit are often rooted in pride, selfish ambition and the desire to look good for man. At times the motivating factor may also be guilt or fear. Keep in mind *"God has not given us the spirit of fear but of power, love and a sound mind."* (2 Timothy 1:7 KJV). God does not drive or motivate His children through fear and guilt. Only a religious spirit from the enemy would seek to do that. Our motivation for serving and doing things for Jesus Christ should be first of all, knowing it is not about us but it is about Jesus and the souls for whom He laid down His life. Another reason should be because we simply love Jesus and the lost, and that is our main passion in life. When our emphasis is doing things for God, rather than being driven by a religious spirit, lasting fruit will be in abundance. Another thing to keep in mind is that Holy Spirit always motivates through love and conviction. The religious spirit motivates through guilt, fear, control and sometimes hype.

Sacrifice vs Obedience

Unfortunately, too much of Christianity is copying what others have done. While this may look good to man, it may not be what God necessarily desires. A religious spirit's focus can be on the past, constricting God to move in exactly the same way. Great attention is given to past moves of the Spirit. Attempts are made to stir up similar events and make similar sacrifices in the hope that God will respond and once again move powerfully. We need to glean from the past but more importantly press onward. We need fresh moves of Holy Spirit, not living on yesterday's manna or victories. It takes people who will press in and are hungry for God, not **just** copying what others have done in the past to see a breakthrough. We need to cease living on yesterday's victories. A new battle rages each day. Souls hang in the balance.

The religious spirit promotes sacrifice over obedience, a contradiction to the Bible, which says in 1 Samuel 15:22, *"...to obey is better than sacrifice..."* The anointing comes from the obedience to God, not just sacrificing. Many times we as Christians put more faith in our ability to sacrifice rather than the promises of God or His grace. We somehow expect the presence of the Lord to increase because of our sacrifices. If we persist in this belief we may witness a few moves of God, but eventually will be disappointed, surrounded by dead works that produce no lasting fruit.

The religious spirit will drive a person to such an extent that they are constantly sacrificing in front of man but are not experiencing the refreshing presence of Holy Spirit. There will be times God calls us to sacrifice but keep in mind obedience is the key. We might be sacrificing in the eyes of other Christians but Jesus is waiting for us to come unto Him (to experience intimacy with him) so he can free us from being overburdened with religious ceremony that robs us of the anointing. If we obey Him even our sacrifice is easy because we are taking on His yoke (task), which He gives us the strength to do. Philippians 4:13 says *"I can do **all things through Christ** who strengthens me."* If He has called us to do something He will strengthen us to do it. Obedience is the ultimate key. The important issue is to hear His voice and be obedient to do what He says. We should not try to limit God in any way. He is far too big and creative to be limited.

It is sad when church services are predictable and dead. Why? The reason is that we are too busy following our own agenda or acting religious to try to work up the Spirit of God, instead of being obedient to His promptings. Obedience = anointing to set the captives free. All that is left when Holy Spirit has departed and we are not following His leading is dead religion.

Hearing His voice when He speaks **comes only through intimacy and communion** with Him. This is the only way that we will ever be able to hear His voice - through intimacy and communion with Him. Also keep in mind God will never call us to do things that are contrary or in disagreement to the Scriptures.

In Luke 10:38-42 we see Martha busy serving while Mary sat at Jesus' feet to hear His word. Martha complained about Mary not serving. Notice Jesus' response: *"Martha, Martha, you are worried and troubled about many things. But one thing is needed, and* **Mary** *has* **chosen that good part,** *which* **will not be taken away** *from her"* (Luke 10:41-42). God desires intimacy and obedience before serving Him. What Mary received through sitting at Jesus' feet could not be taken away from her. Religion and acting religious will rob us of the anointing and revelation that comes directly from Heaven.

Do not get busy just serving Jesus without knowing Him intimately first. The anointing comes from the times we spend hearing His voice and being in His presence. Pursue Him more than the anointing, gifts, power, recognition, etc and you will have all you need in life to succeed. Why? Because it is found in Him.

CHAPTER 5

Laying Aside the Commands of God

Mark 7:8 says *"For **laying aside the commandment of God, you hold the tradition of men** - the washing of pitchers and cups, and many other such things you do."* Notice how concisely Jesus outlines the religious spirit's progression from fault finding, to arrogance, to laying aside the commands of God. The commands of God become null and void in the life of those governed by the religious spirit.

What is the primary command of the Lord? Mark 12:30 says *"And you shall love the Lord your God with all your heart, with all your soul and with all your mind, and with all your strength. This is the first commandment. And the second, like it, is this: you shall love your neighbor as yourself. There is no other commandment greater than these."* Jesus also says in love all the Law and the commandments are fulfilled. The Old Testament laws and commandments need to be fulfilled; but if we spend more time teaching the law rather than **teaching grace and practicing love** then it will be difficult to keep the Ten Commandments. Why? Because instilling a sin consciousness will not help live free from sin. Teaching people love, grace and who they are in Christ will help live free from sin.

If we exhort people to understand grace and practice love, even if they do not know the Ten Commandments, there exists the great probability that they will not break the Ten Commandments. The reason being that the grace of God and the love of God that they walk in, will keep them from doing so. Galatians 5:13-14 says *"For you, brethren, have been called to liberty; only do not use liberty as an opportunity for the flesh, but through love serve one another. For the **Law is fulfilled in one word,** even in this: You shall love your neighbor as yourself."*

The Old Testament law focuses on the outside of the man, while the New Testament focuses on the inside or the heart of man. I have a question for you. If I am trying to disciple and help a new believer walk with God, should I teach him about the judgment of God or the **goodness of God?** Undeniably the goodness of God! Romans 2:4 puts it this way, *"Or do you despise the **riches of His goodness,** forbearance, and long-suffering,* not knowing that **the goodness of God leads you to repentance.**" When we teach on the goodness of God, then people will not want to sin.

Spirit of Love – vs – Doom and Gloom

"*They shall utter the memory of Your great goodness, And shall sing of Your righteousness. The LORD IS GRACIOUS AND FULL OF COMPASSION, SLOW TO ANGER AND GREAT IN MERCY. THE LORD IS GOOD TO ALL, And His tender mercies are over all His works*" (Psalms 145:7-9). From these verses we see that God is full of compassion and slow to anger. If we are motivated by Holy Spirit those who are around us will be encouraged and motivated to serve God because of His love and goodness.

There are many Christians who are prone to arguing and debating scriptures constantly. Others usually avoid such individuals because there is a heaviness upon them. This is nothing more than a religious spirit of strife. If these people would take the time to understand they would realize most people do not like to be around Christians who love to argue and debate scriptures. Neither does God (See Proverbs 6:16-19).

There are many Christians who teach solely on the anger and judgment of God. Their concept of God is that He is always angry. They carry a spirit of heaviness and gloom. Whenever something looks bleak they come along and quickly prophecy judgment, doom and gloom.

A good example was all the doom and gloom predicted during 1999, concerning Y2K. Aka as Y2Nothing. Many Christian leaders forecasted great problems in 2000. Their opinion was "this is God's judgment" for one reason or the other. The hands of the clock took us from 1999 to 2000, and nothing unusual occurred. Unfortunately most of these prophets of doom and gloom did not publicly repent for missing God and creating such hysteria. Instead we probably will be hearing of more doom and gloom when they get another opportunity. This is how a religious spirit motivates people: through fear, guilt, condemnation, hype and heaviness. A religious spirt will also beat up Christians with guilt and shame from their past even though God forgave them.

1 Corinthians 14:3 says *"But he who prophesies speaks edification and exhortation and comfort to men."* 1 Corinthians 14:26 says *"... let all things be done for* **edification** (Greek- **building up**). The test of a true Prophet is they here *"for the equipping of the saints for the work of the ministry, for the **edifying** (Greek- **building up**) of the Body of Christ"* (Ephesians 4:12). If they are not edifying and building up other Christians, then

they are operating in a religious spirit.

To properly discern if something is from God or not, we need to test the spirit behind it. Is it a **voice of concern and compassion** or is it a religious critical spirit speaking to bring people into condemnation, fear, hype and control? The Old Testament prophets spoke with love and concern, saying that God's will was for his people to repent and not to have to face the coming judgment.

Many times those bound by a religious spirit are prophesying through their own distorted concept of God. It results from negative experiences, offenses or a critical spirit. They cannot comprehend God as a God of Love, but rather one who is waiting to judge and punish us. Therefore they are constantly conversing on and prophesying negative things that are far from the heart of God. Unless repentance comes, when they miss God; they will continue to prophesy by a deceptive religious spirit, leading people astray. Ask God for the gift of discerning of spirits (see 1 Corinthians 12:10) so that you may know when this religious spirit is in operation.

There are many self-proclaimed prophets out there with no accountability to anyone, operating with a spirit of heaviness, nothing more than a religious spirit. Paul said in 1 Corinthians 14 32-33 says *And the spirits of the prophets are subject to the prophets. For God is not the author of confusion but of peace, as in all the churches of the saints.*

In Luke 9:51-56 we see how a Samaritan village did not receive Christ. James and John (the sons of thunder) wanted to call fire down from heaven and consume them. Jesus rebuked them and said ***"You do not know what manner or spirit you are of.*** *For the son of Man did not come to destroy men's lives but to save them"* (Luke 9:55-56). They were operating by the same religious spirit that drove the Pharisees and Sadducees. Today we have many in Christian circles operating by that same spirit. God's heart is in restoration and love.

Many Christians are somehow sidetracked and constantly talking about how the judgment of God or how God will be pouring out his wrath on countries because of all the sin. They need to keep things in mind. One is that God the Father did judge our sin. It was judged 2,000 years ago at Calvary as His only Son hung suspended, bleeding and dying between heaven and earth to pay the price of our sin. *For He made Him who knew no sin to be sin for us, that we might become the righteousness of God in Him* (2 Corinthians 5:21). His wrath was poured out at Calvary. Now we operate under His grace and righteousness. We get good things from Him we do not deserve and things we could never work up through our good deeds.

If you study the time Jesus walked this earth perversion, corruption and sin were running rampant. All you have to do is study a little history from that time. Bill O'Reilly's book **Killing Jesus** is a great book to read of the history of that time. Yet Jesus said *For God so loved the world that He gave His only begotten Son, that whoever believes in Him should not perish but have everlasting life. For God* **did not send His Son into the world to condemn the world,** *but that* **the world through Him might be saved** (John 3:16-17). If there ever were people who deserved the judgement and wrath of God, the Romans and Jewish religious leaders of that time deserved it but instead they had the Creator of the universe come down in love, to serve and to lay down His life as a ransom and absorb the judgement and wrath of God for us. Jesus said *"Just as the Son of Man did not come to be served, but to serve, and to give His life a ransom for many"* (Matthew 20:28).

If God already judged our sin at Calvary what happens to those who continue to blatantly sin in the eyes of God. Galatians 6:7-8 says *Do not be deceived, God is not mocked; for whatever a man sows, that he will also reap. For he who sows to his flesh will of the flesh reap corruption, but he who sows to the Spirit will of the Spirit reap everlasting life.* There is a universal law of sowing and reaping established from the beginning of time (see Genesis 8:22). Many times we reap what we sow, but sometimes the grace of God covers us and we do not get what we deserve. We run headlong into His goodness and mercy. Does that mean we continue in sin? *What shall we say then? Shall we continue in sin that grace may abound? Certainly not! How shall we who died to sin live any longer in it* (Romans 6:1-2)? Romans 6:16 says *Do you not know that to whom you present yourselves slaves to obey, you are that one's slaves whom you obey, whether of sin leading to death, or of obedience leading to righteousness?*

2 Peter 2:19 says *While they promise them liberty, they themselves are slaves of corruption; for by whom a person is overcome, by him also he is brought into bondage.* So who is bringing about these terrible circumstances? We do. We bring individual judgment on ourselves but don't blame God. He is not the one doing it.

Who is doing it? Repeated sin opens the door to the demonic realm. Demons have free access to us when we open up to them. God is not bringing judgement on us but we bring it on ourselves by opening up to the demonic realm. Also keep in mind just because bad things happen to us does not mean God is doing it or bringing judgement on us. We live in a fallen depraved world. Some things we can not explain and we will not figure out in this lifetime.

Job 2:7 says *So Satan went out from the presence of the Lord, and struck Job with painful boils from the sole of his foot to the crown of his head.* Throughout the book of Job you will see Job blaming God for His problems and thinking God was doing this evil to him. Finally at the end of Job in Job 4:8 (Moffatt) God says to Job *To justify yourself, will you condemn Me?* Job was blaming the wrong person. He never once realized there was a Satan or demons doing the oppressing, bringing all these misfortunes on him. Job was the first book written in the Bible. He lived long before the time of Moses. He did not walk in the revelation or have access to the revelation we can walk in today, since Jesus went to Calvary.

Job all along thought that was God was the oppressor. How many Christians do the same thing with God, accusing Him of doing both good and bad because of a gravitation towards Job's theology over Christ's theology? When corrected by God Job humbled himself, repented, forgave his friends and was blessed with twice as much (see Job 42:10). Did God allow Job to be afflicted? Yes He did! But He was not the one oppressing Job, doing evil to him and bringing judgement on him.

Denying the Power of God

The religious leaders laid aside the command of love. They had no love in their heart. They broke the first and foremost command of the Lord in its stead they followed the doctrines and traditions of man. 2 Timothy 3:5 warns us against such people, *"Having a form of godliness but denying its power. And from such people turn away."* Let us not be people who only have a form of godliness, but lack in the important areas of manifesting the love and power of God. The unsaved world needs to see the love and power of God as opposed to a form of godliness. When we lay aside the commands of God to follow the traditions of men, in essence we are laying aside the love and power of God.

I highly recommend doing a study of the book of **Galatians**. In this book Paul deals with the bondage of the religious spirit, legalism, and dead works in the Body of Christ. *"O foolish Galatians! Who has bewitched you that you should not obey the truth, before whose eyes Jesus Christ was clearly portrayed among you as crucified? This only I want to learn from you: Did you receive the Spirit by the works of the law, or by the hearing of faith? Are you so foolish? Having begun in the Spirit, are you now being made perfect by the flesh? Have ye suffered so many things in vain? if it be yet in vain. Therefore He who supplies the Spirit to you and **works miracles** among you, does He do it by the works of law, or **by the hearing of faith"** (Galatians 3:1-5)? Verse 4 states that when we do things because of legalism and dominated by a works mentality, as opposed to operating in the grace of God, we are doing them in vain and we suffer many things in vain.

Whatever we accomplish for the Lord is done through faith rather than the law. Often we may think that in order to see someone healed we need to say long and loud prayers, or maybe we need to yell and shake, or the person needs to fall down. This is not necessarily true. Often in our campaigns overseas and even here in the USA, just the mention of the name of Jesus spoken in authority over the sick heals them. We cannot work up the power of God. It comes through knowing Holy Spirit intimately, operating in authority, through faith and by God's grace.

Sign of Holy Spirit Moving?

In the early days of this ministry I thought that if people were **slain in the spirit** (falling under the power of God), then God was moving upon them. My desires were thus directed towards that - seeing people fall under the power of God during my ministry time. I was greatly inspired by what I saw in Benny Hinn's ministry. This would occur often when I would minister, but most people were not healed. My ego also stood in the way because I wanted to impress people with how many would be slain as I prayed. I then realized, that the power was not necessarily in being "slain." I hence changed my desires and asked the Lord to simply heal the sick (see Mark 16:17). Since then a tremendous number of people have been healed of all kinds of ailments, most of them without being 'slain in the spirit.'

Please understand, I am not opposed to being slain in the spirit, we have seen many fall and even fly through the air as God's power came on them. What I am wary of is when it becomes a necessity or proof of successful ministry. Many think a sign of a true move of God is seeing people slain in the Spirit. There is a lot more to the anointing than merely being slain. In fact there is nothing in the scripture that indicates this was a practice of the early church. Falling out under the power of God happened in the Bible at times but they did not practice this as proof they were anointed.

Many Christians have used being slain in the spirit as a barometer to decide whether God is moving or not. Thus some are simply falling out even when it is not God doing it. They do it this way to try to work up the power of Holy Spirit. It is nothing more than hype. If you are going to fall out under the power of God why not let God do it? We do not need people purposely falling down or need to push people to the floor. Holy Spirit does not need our help.

Rejecting the Commandments of God

*"He said to them, All too well **you reject the commandments of God,** that you may **keep your tradition"** (Mark 7:9). The more

we give place to the religious spirit, the more we come to the place that it is not just laying aside the commands of God, but ultimately rejecting them. I do not need to speak much about this. This verse speaks for itself. When a person continues to operate by a religious spirit it will eventually lead to rejecting the commands of God to follow man made traditions.

Mark 7:10-13 says *"For Moses said, Honor your father and mother; and he who curses father or mother, let him be put to death. But you say. If a man says to his father or mother, whatever profit you might have received from me is Corban -* (that is, a gift to God), *then you no longer let him do anything for his father or his mother,* **making the word of God of no effect through your tradition** *which you have handed down. And many such things you do."*

One of the commandments is to honor your father and mother. Even this commandment was changed by the religious leaders of Jesus' day to suit their own ends. **They perverted the Word of God in order to keep their own traditions and to suit themselves in order to follow their own agenda and to control the people.** As a result the word of God had no effect in their life because of their man made traditions and rejection of God's commands. Unfortunately today many have come to the place where the Word of God is taught or preached and it has absolutely no effect on the people. We know God's word does not return void (see Isaiah 55:10-11) unless the religious spirit has progressed to this stage.

In a recent survey Christians were asked if they discovered that a doctrine they had been taught in church, or the way they believed was contrary to scripture what would they do. Most Christians choose religious traditions over the Word of God. The root of this is arrogance and pride, which God resists.

Adornment – to set in Order First

As people give place to the religious spirit, I have seen them misinterpret or pervert scripture to substantiate their own traditions. One of the most misinterpreted scriptures in many of the countries like India, in Central and South America, I have traveled to is 1 Peter 3:3-4, *"Do not let your **adornment be merely outward** - arranging the hair, wearing gold, or putting on fine apparel- **rather** let it be the hidden person of the heart, with the incorruptible beauty of a gentle and quiet spirit, which is very precious in the sight of God."* I have seen women put into bondage as a result of a misuse of these scriptures in many parts of the world, because the religious spirit dominated their leaders and an unnecessary emphasis was put on the outward appearance.

As a new Christian my wife was a victim of this legalism. The pastor of the church she attended as a new believer was completely against the idea of women wearing make-up, jewelry or jeans and enforced his decisions and ideas on her. She was told continually that she was sinning because she outwardly adorned herself, she wore jeans or dressed nicely. She felt guilty because she enjoyed dressing well and looking good. Gradually she stopped attending church and ultimately backslid for a period of time. Unfortunately, in such cases the focus is more on the outside rather than the heart of the person.

If we are to bring about lasting change it will come by teaching people and new believers who they are in Christ. The inside or heart of a person needs to be changed first, because that is what is important to God, not how a person dresses, or their outward appearance. When a person's heart is right with God he/she will not want to sin and will make any necessary changes in their appearance that are truly pleasing to God.

Adornment comes from the Greek word that means to '**set in order first.**' Let us now read 1 Peter 3:3 replacing adornment with the Greek alternative. *"Do **not set in order first** the arranging of the hair, wearing gold or putting on fine apparel- rather let it be the hidden person of the heart..."* It is also imperative that we interpret these scriptures in the context that they were written. At that time women were focusing more on their outward appearance rather than the inward and this is what Peter was addressing. To reiterate God does not care what we do with the outside, what He really cares about is the condition of the heart. **We need to set in order first our heart.** What we do to fix up or not fix up the outside does not matter to God. He leaves that up to our own personal taste and preference.

Other Perversions of God's Word

Another perversion or misinterpretation of scripture is how many Christians refer to themselves as *"just sinners saved by grace."* 2 Corinthians 5:21 says *For he hath made him to be sin for us, who knew no sin; that we might be made the righteousness of God in him.* I was a **sinner** (someone who practiced sin), I am now the righteousness of God because of Jesus Christ. Jesus made me worthy of His best.

Our own righteousness, as a way to seek right standing with God, is as filthy rags (Isaiah 64:6). I am not living my life based on my own righteousness, but on Christ's. He has made me worthy and righteous! *Even the **righteousness of God,** through faith in Jesus Christ, **to all and on all who believe. For there is no difference; for all have sinned** and fall short of the glory of God* (Romans 3:22-23). All have sinned and because all have sinned all can be made righteous by the shed blood of Jesus Christ. If we still consider ourselves sinners, we are saying what Jesus did 2000 years ago was not enough.

1 John 3:8 says *He who* sins (Greek-**practices sin**) *is of the*

*devil, for the devil sinned from the beginning. For this purpose the son of God was manifested, **to destroy the works of the devil.*** Jesus was manifested to destroy sin, sickness, demonic control and poverty in our life (see also Galatians 3:13-14). When He said *"it is finished"* while hanging on the cross He finished destroying the works of the devil over your life. That includes the sin we once had in our lives!

Examples of the Religious Spirit

As a young man I was working in a factory, when one rude man, a recent Bible College graduate came up to me to share the **gospel (good news**). He thought that because I had somewhat long hair I could not be a Christian despite my passion to bring people to Christ. He handed me a tract entitled, '**Can a Man with Long Hair be Saved**' and another tract telling me I was going to hell because I spoke in tongues. We will not win people to Christ if we focus on the outside more than the inside of an individual. People need to change internally, and then if the outside needs change, it can be accomplished. Dealing with internal issues will cause us to see lasting change in the lives of those we minister to. God's main concern is our heart attitude.

My wife has shared some sad stories with me regarding the behavior of Christians in her homeland, India. A leading respected minister in India invited a Christian woman and her nominal believing Hindu husband over to supper. The minister and his wife did not eat with them because they refused to eat with a Hindu. He had them eat in a different room. What would Jesus have done in a situation like that? He was accused of being a **friend of sinners** many times by the religious leaders of His day. Did Jesus eat with sinners? Yes He did!

What would the Apostle Paul have done? Paul said in 1 Corinthians 9:22 ... *"I have become **all things to all men,** that I might by all means save some."* This Hindu man was interested in becoming a Christian during that time but because of that situation we was turned off to Christianity. This minister's legalism became a stumbling block to this Hindu man believing in Christ. This kind of religious spirit is all over in Christian circles in India. It is an attitude that says, "I am better than you." God hates this elitist attitude in Christians.

2 Corinthians 6:17 says *"Come out from among them and be separate, says the Lord, Do not touch what is unclean, and I will receive you."* Many Christians have taken this scripture to an extreme by saying they had to be separated from sinners. All we have to do is look at the life of Jesus and the Apostle Paul to understand that this scripture is not telling us to avoid sinners, but on the contrary to be a light to them. How else will they be saved? We are to separate ourselves from the world's evil ways,

but we are part of this world to reach the lost by our example of serving and loving them to Christ.

2 Chronicles 16:9 says *"For the eyes of the Lord run to and fro throughout the whole earth, to show Himself strong on behalf of those **whose heart is loyal to Him...**"* Thus I have no qualms in boldly stating that what we wear or do not wear, the length of our hair, or the jewelry we wear will not affect our salvation. Ultimately it is our personal relationship with Jesus Christ and the state of our heart that matters to Jesus. Do not get caught up in giving place to a religious spirit. It will destroy your fellowship with God and keep you from being successful in your Christian walk and ministry. It may also drive others away from Christ.

In conclusion I would like to mention that in the Gospels not once do we read of a Pharisee, confronted in his stronghold of legalism and self-righteousness, ever admit to seeing it in himself. My point is that no one is likely to see himself/herself with a religious attitude and/or spirit without an honest, penetrating and courageous look inside. Let each one of us be open to search his own heart and get rid of any leaven of the Pharisees and Sadducees. It will help make us the End Time Warrior Christ has called us to be.

PART II
The Great Effects of Relationship

CHAPTER 6

Humility and the Glory

One of the most important ingredients to keep the atmosphere conducive for miracles, healings, signs, wonders and a lasting move of God is Christlike humility! We shared about this in Chapter 3. I will be sharing some things from my book **Humility the Hidden Key to Walking in Signs and Wonders** and from Pastor Steve C. Shank's (www.stevecshank.com) excellent book **God Made Visible, Seeing His Glory and Experiencing His Presence.** Why humility? Humility is the key ingredient that brings His glory into our midst. It should be our deepest cry just like Moses to say *show me your glory* (Exodus 33:18). Without His glory all we have is lifeless religion at best.

So what is the Glory? There are two meanings to the word

glory. One is the manifestation of the Glory of God, which means an exhibition of, the excellence, or greatness of His manifested presence here is the physical realm. It is heaven or the living Christ being manifested and seen within our midst. Something glorious commands our attention. The second meaning is the honor, the fame and the praise due His name. When we take credit for the good things He does, somehow thinking we made it happen we are robbing God of the glory due Him. *Not that we are sufficient of ourselves to think of anything as being from ourselves, but our sufficiency is from God* (2 Corinthians 3:5). When glory goes to God from a heart full of thankfulness His glory descends on this earth. When our glory or glory of man comes on the scene eventually His glory lifts. The main thing that terminates great moves of God and prevents the manifestation of His glory is arrogance, the glory of man.

There have been tremendous moves of God throughout out church history. Most have been short-lived. Why? Proverbs 16:18 gives us the answer. *Pride goes before destruction, and a haughty spirit before a fall* (Proverbs 16:18). If we would only take time to learn from all those who failed this test we would not be repeating the same mistake time and time again. We need to learn to steward the anointing for His glory only.

One reason Sharmila and I were ordained, licensed and came under the covering of Randy Clark and Bill Johnson's ministry is the humility they walk in. Randy Clark is known for being used by God in the Toronto outpouring that occurred over 20 years ago and has only increased since the initial outpouring. Millions have come into the Kingdom of God and many hundreds of people raised from the dead (maybe thousands) in this outpouring. Randy wrote the forward in my book **Humility The Hidden Key to Walking in Signs and Wonders.** Here is what he said about humility being so very important in relation to the great outpouring that spread worldwide out of Toronto. Holy Spirit spoke this to him just before going to Toronto. Randy's words *"I will never forget the message's meaning: "This is the most dangerous moment of your life. If you touch the glory, become proud, fail to stay humble, this anointing will destroy you."* I have watched in my lifetime one minister after another fall because they did not understand or comprehend these words spoken to Randy before Holy Spirit began to use Him so powerfully throughout the world. I have watched the very anointing that came on them, using them so powerfully at one time, eventually destroy them. You can not mix the glory of God with the glory of man. It spells disaster.

I do believe followers of Jesus are catching on, that in order to see a lasting move of God and His glory (heaven) manifested on the earth humility is a priority. In India and Nepal I have shared this principle time and time again with leaders who work with us. Now Holy Spirit is using them powerfully. At times I have to sit back and let Jesus' glory manifest through them, even though I am the main speaker. As a result some of these leaders like **Pastor Ankit Sajwan** and others are seeing awesome miracles such as hopeless cripples instantly healed, blind eyes deaf ears opened, cancer and tumors supernaturally disappearing and even the dead raised in their ministry. Pastor Ankit will be featured in an upcoming movie entitled: **Christ in You the Movie** due out December 2016.

On a consistent basis in our outreaches Jesus and or angels have been appearing to Hindus and Muslims and they have been supernaturally healed or delivered. Many times this happened when **Sam Sean** our worship leader in India was leading people into heartfelt worship. The glory of God descended on the crowd. I don't get up and speak as I would quench immediately what Holy Spirit was doing. I will let my wife Sharmila share about one of those times.

SUNDERNAGAR, INDIA, Spring 2013, Report by Sharmila Anderson

MANY SEE JESUS AND ANGELS! HAVE MIRACULOUS ENCOUNTERS!

Sundernagar, *nestled deep in the Himalaya Mountains is surrounded by Hindu temples. Its claim to fame in India is the millions of pilgrims who visit the numerous temples throughout the year hoping to be cleansed of their sins. Almost every person we met was named after a Hindu god or goddess. Practically untouched by Christian witness the few pastors and leaders of the area had prayed for 4 years for the Lord to send someone who would help them reach the unreached and train the local believers. Did the Lord ever answer those prayers... He sent the best of the best.....* *Holy Spirit invaded Sundernagar in an explosion of love and grace that we have never witnessed before. We stood in awe as He revealed Himself to Hindus visibly, freeing them of demonic torment, healing bodies, freeing them to dance for Him, baptizing them with fire and on and on. We were humbled by what we saw, the sheer beauty of His presence and what His love does to people. It is so hard to put into words what we experienced in Sundernagar and I know that I will fall short... still I will try!*

The first night Mark asked the gathered crowd (mostly Hindu) if they were willing to invite Jesus and Holy Spirit into their city. The crowd willing stood to their feet and welcomed Jesus and Holy Spirit into their midst. This was the beginning of 2 days of pure, uninhibited worship unto Him. I think all the unsaved who attended accepted Jesus as Lord and Savior.

The first night many women manifested with demons, screaming, rolling on the ground, jumping like monkeys, hitting themselves, it was a pitiful sight to behold.

*A Hindu man **Bikram Singh,** had a vision of Jesus on the Cross with blood flowing down. After that he saw Jesus moving through the crowd touching people during the mass prayer for healing. Many people were instantly healed by the presence of Holy Spirit that night. He and his wife wore Hindu charms to ward off evil spirits. They removed their Hindu charms of their own accord. Mark prayed over him. His short leg came out and his back was instantly healed right where he had worn his Hindu charm previously.*

***Shalu** had a miscarriage as her uterus was out of place. She felt a hand move it into place. **Jyoti** had to be carried to the meeting as she had been ill for months and could not walk. Her legs had turned blue. During prayer she was instantly energized by Holy Spirit and walked up and testified.*

***Sushma's** story struck a deep cord with me. Sushma a lady in her twenties, had been married into a Hindu family. After her marriage her parents and Sushma came to Christ. In her in-laws home Sushma was obligated to perform the religious rituals which brought on severe demonic torment. If she refused to do so she would be turned out of the house and being a poor person would have no way to take care of herself. As it is since accepting Christ her life* with her husband was not good for her. I ministered to her for a long time as she rolled in the dirt, banged her bare feet and head on the ground, slammed her hands on the ground breaking the glass bangles she wore that cut into her skin causing deep gashes and bleeding. Her mother was distraught over her daughter's condition. Later that evening Mark and I prayed that an angel would be sent to protect Sushma and she would find freedom.

The second night our worship leader **Samarpan Sean** led us into worship that invited Holy Spirit. As everyone worshipped Mark asked if anyone had an encounter with Jesus or angels or was healed as result of that. Hands went up all over the gathering and then we heard the most marvelous things as people came up and testified of their experiences. The pastors wife saw a vision of a ball of fire roll into the tent and then flames began to shoot out of the ball landing on the people in the tent. She said that she had never had a vision before.

Sushma, who was manifesting with demons the night before was the second person who testified that night. She could barely speak and was shaking uncontrollably as she testified of seeing an angel whose head reached the top of the tent. She experienced severe heat and coolness after the angel touched her during the time Mark was saying some of you are experiencing a heat in your body and at the same time a coolness. She was instantly set free.

We watched **Ranvir** shaking during worship. He testified that he saw a very handsome man in a white robe with longish hair on the stage smiling and waving to him. It was Jesus. Later his mother who also had a supernatural encounter said that her son, Ranvir was a very troubled youth. Seeing Jesus waving at him, we asked Ranvir what did that make you feel like. He said he wanted to go hang out with Jesus.

Mala Devi, a widow, with no children, was dying of breast cancer. She had come to Sundernagar to visit the temples, to try the appease the Hindu gods before she died. She wandered from one Hindu temple to another finding no peace. We ran buses around the city to bring people to our outreach. Someone invited her and she came out to the meeting. She knew nothing of Jesus and His love. She said that during worship she fell down. She thought someone had pushed her. Then she felt an unseen hand lift her up. It was Jesus. She had been suffering with breast cancer and she felt the oozing in her breasts stop. She told that she had just heard of Jesus, and he had taken away all her fear. She knew that even though she had no one Jesus would take care of her. She said that now she had no fear of death as she knew she would be with Jesus. She was full of joy.

Mansa Devi had a stomach operation that was a failure. She suffered with constant seeping from her stomach, was always in pain and very tired. She saw angels and felt the seeping in her stomach cease instantly. **Neha** was completely blind in one eye. She saw a bright light and instantly her blind eye saw. **Ritika**, a young girl had been praying for her mother who had stones in the kidneys and was scheduled for an operation. Ritika experienced extreme heat and began to speak in tongues and her mother felt the stones dissolve.

The number of people testifying was endless. We had to finally stop taking any more testimonies. One lady saw Jesus in the midst of a rainbow and began to speak in tongues. Many spoke in tongues having no idea what it was. Jesus was seen by some with a crown of thorns, others beheld Him with the crown of a king, while some saw a pillar of fire in the midst of the tent. These were Hindus who had never heard about Him, yet their descriptions of Him lined up with Scripture. Some experienced severe heat, others coolness and some both. Please keep in mind that all this happened before Mark preached and many of the attendees who had encounters with Jesus had never heard about Him.

Bikram Singh who saw a vision of Jesus on the cross the prior night attended the second night also. He and his wife had removed their Hindu charms the night before. Later as Mark sang the **"Ultimate Sacrifice"** she danced a beautiful dance in the Spirit. She did not know English yet her movements mimicked what Mark sang. Later as I conversed with her she told me that as Mark began to sing she saw a tall man standing by Him with a crown and she felt compelled to dance. She said that she could never have done such a thing on her own whim as she is very timid and shy.

A young newly married lady brought her sister-in-law and nephew (infant) to me requesting prayer. The mother had put a black spot on his face to ward off evil spirits. As I began to tell her that with Jesus she did not have to worry for her child's safety, the young bride bean to tell her that the blood of Jesus was sufficient protection and Jesus would take care and heal them amongst other things. Impressed I asked her how long she had been with Jesus. Her answer amazed me. She had heard about Jesus the night before and accepted Him as Lord. She said that she felt like someone was explaining things to her about Jesus and opening the Scriptures to her.

People were willingly removing charms and fetishes that they wore. It was so beautiful to behold Jesus loving His precious people who were so lost without Him and the way they embraced Him with open arms. As the crowds were smaller, I was able to visit a number of people after the meetings. I learned that they were predominantly Hindus who were hearing about Jesus for the first time and they attended because of the buses we ran that came to their areas to pick them up and bring them back a forth to the meetings. One lady told me she was just going about her day with her brother when the bus came to her neighborhood. Her brother refused to go, and she *too did not really want to come, but came half heartedly as she had nothing else to do. She had a visual encounter with Jesus and was healed too. She was so happy that she had come!*

In all, in two days we saw about 375 first time decisions made for Christ in this city. In a follow up conversation a few days later my mother asked the pastor who hosted us for some feedback. He was still shook up from what the Lord had done. He said his church alone has added 35 people the Sunday after we left. All new believers! He had received phone calls from villages asking him to come and minister to the new believers. He has invited us to Sundernagar again next year..." Check out **Jesus and Angels Appear in Sundanagar, India** at www.markandersonministries.com/category/videos.

The following year, 2014, I returned to Sundernagar. Many people were healed, saved and saw Jesus and or angels face to face once again. We also did another outreach during that trip in Kullu, Himachal Pradesh, India. In all 1,900 people came to Christ on that trip. This was in the state of Himachal Pradesh India. This is the state Hindus believe their gods originated from. There is only one Christian for every 1,100 people in this militant Hindu controlled state. Check out: **North India May 2014 Trip** at www.markandersonministries.com/category/videos.

While in Sundernagar Spring of 2014 I met **Mr. and Mrs. Bikram Singh** once again. Both had accepted Jesus in our first outreach. I asked them how life was since they began to serve Jesus. Mrs. Singh is now a passionate worshipper of Christ. She told me that on a regular basis when they sit down to eat their evening meal Jesus appears and has dinner with them. When I think about what she shared, many times it has brought me to tears and sometimes I have a hard time speaking. The more we glorify Jesus Christ from our heart the more His glory manifests on earth. That is when people have a heart to worship and are not just going through the mechanics of worship. The more people rob the glory from Jesus the more the anointing dissipates.

Jesus said *Come unto **Me**, all you who labor and are **heavy laden**, and I will give you **rest**. **Take My yoke** upon you and **learn from Me**, for I am **gentle and lowly in heart**, and you will find rest for your souls. For **My yoke is easy** and My burden is light* (Matthew 11:28-30).

In these verses, Jesus very clearly explains His character and nature. In verse 28, He invites the heavy laden to come to Him and find rest. The word for *heavy laden* in the Greek means to *load up, to overburden with ceremony or spiritual anxiety.* Many Christians are just going through religious motions, feeling overburdened, and producing little or no fruit. When we come unto Him, He says He will give us rest from that. The Greek brings it out this way: He will give *"recreation, intermission, pause, and a letting down of chords drawn tight."* Serving Jesus in India and Nepal has become like recreation for us. Ministry for Him is easy and so very enjoyable because we do not have to work it up.

In verse 29 Jesus tells us to take His yoke (Greek: *obligation*) upon us and learn from Him. What does He want us to learn? Think about this, if you learn something directly from the heart of Jesus, it will be more than just head knowledge. You experience something that will radically change your life. What will we learn from Him? *"I am gentle and lowly in heart or **I am humble."*** Nowhere else does Jesus make a statement quite like this. He is letting us know that humility is what He is all about. *"I am Humble!"* Most people have misconceptions of what humility is. As a result of the misconception humility has not been a priority in the Body of Christ. Why? Most people, including most Christians think of humility wrongly. They think the more humble you are the more poor you will be. When they think of humility they think a humble person is someone who is insecure, timid, shy, weak, a coward, a yes person, a doormat, and not someone who will not accomplish much in life. Jesus said I am humble. Was he any of those negative things?

Was He poor? *For you know the grace of our Lord Jesus Christ, that though He was rich, yet for your sakes He became poor, that you through His poverty might become rich* (2 Corinthians 8:9). Jesus was rich yet He became poor for us. When did He become poor? Not when was he was born! What happened when He was born? Wise men came and laid gold, myrrh and frankincense at His manger. If you were rich in Jesus' days that is exactly what you had. He became poor when He gave it all up and went to Calvary. In fact Jesus was HUMILITY IN ITS PUREST FORM come down from Heaven. Humility does not bring poverty like religious tradition of man began teaching us around 400AD. It brings riches and honor. *By **humility** and the fear of the Lord are **riches and honor** and life* (Proverbs 22:4). Humility is a wealth magnet, not so we are consumed by riches or wealth consumers, but so we can be wealth generators for the sake of the Gospel. In the days to come you will be seeing this more and more in the Body of Christ as people grab hold of humility from the heart.

Was Jesus insecure? No! Then from where does insecurity come? It comes from pride and the glory of man. Proverbs 11:2 **When pride comes, then comes shame;** *But with the humble is wisdom.* A byproduct of pride is shame and insecurity. Was Jesus timid, shy, cowardly or weak? No! Look at His boldness even in the face of death and persecution from the religious leaders. From where does shyness and timidity come? It comes from pride when we are more concerned about our reputation and what people think of us than Christ's reputation. Pride can cause us to be bound with the fear of man.

Let this mind be in you which was also in Christ Jesus, who, being in the form of God, did not consider it robbery to be equal with God, **but made Himself of no reputation,** *taking the form of a bondservant, and coming in the likeness of men. And being found in appearance as a man, He humbled Himself and became obedient to the point of death, even the death of the cross. Therefore God also has highly exalted Him and given Him the name which is above every name, that at the name of Jesus every knee should bow, of those in heaven, and of those on earth, and of those under the earth, and that every tongue should confess that Jesus Christ is Lord,* **to the glory of God the Father** (Philippians 2:5-11).

Verse 7 says Jesus made Himself of **no reputation.** Who's reputation and image are you more concerned with yours or His? The Greek word for **no reputation** is Kenosis, which means *to make void, of none effect, laid aside equality with God, deprive of force, cause a thing to be seen to be empty, hollow.* What was it like for God the Creator to strip Himself of who He is, come to earth a man and humble Himself as a servant, even to the point of death itself? **It was the greatest act of humility**

and it led to the greatest exaltation ever (see verse 9-11).

Why humility? How did mankind fall in the beginning of time? Lucifer got lifted up with pride and wanted to be exalted above God (see Ezekiel 28:11-19 & Isaiah 14:12-16). He failed and fell because of His arrogance so he came to earth. On earth he came to destroy God's creation, telling Adam and Eve they could have their eyes opened and be just like God. Adam and Eve yielded to the temptation of pride and fell. That was called the 'PRIDE OF LIFE' (see 1 John 2:16). They fell because of pride. How would mankind be redeemed? BY THE GREATEST ACT OF HUMILITY EVER! God Himself coming to earth in humility would redeem mankind. This is why we need to emphasize humility. **Mankind started this thing with pride and arrogance. Now we are called to finish with humility.**

If we can learn this what would happen to this lost and dying world? The glory of God would cover and be seen all over the world. You might think that is impossible. Look what Habakkuk 2:14 says *For the earth shall be filled with the knowledge of the glory of the Lord, as the waters cover the sea.* Don't question this! Pursue it!

Therefore humble yourselves under the mighty hand of God, that He may exalt you in due time (1 Peter 5:6). Humility means to get low or to be bowed down. Learn from Jesus the way up is to get low.

When I first received my call into ministry in 1978 I was looking for open doors to preach and launch 'my ministry.' It was not taking off as I was hoping it would. In those days I spent a lot of time praying and seeking the Lord but I was full of pride. Finally I received a call to speak in Wisconsin accompanied by my friend, Country Gospel Singer John Peterson. When we arrived at the location the people looked at me and said "You're not Mark Anderson!" There was another Mark Anderson connected with the same Mega Church in Minneapolis that I attended.

Mark is now a leader in Youth with a Mission and various other ministries. These people thought I was him when they invited me to speak. I thought to myself they have the right Mark Anderson. As the meeting started my friend John, a great singer got up and sang. I thought he needed a little help so I got up and helped him out. Not good in those days! Finally it came time to preach. I was already becoming a legend in my own mind and ready to give it to them. The leaders then asked if they could speak to me in side room. I said sure, wondering what it was all about. They said "we do not want you to speak tonight." I asked them why. They said "we see to much pride in your life."

I was greatly offended. Pride will always walk in offense. One of the biggest manifestations of pride and arrogance is the critical spirt and offense.

Holy Spirit was speaking in those days telling me 'this is not about you Mark, but is all about Jesus.' Pride kept me blinded and from listening. For many years after that despite having a strong call into ministry it was a constant up and down rollercoaster and struggle to get the ministry going. Why? Because I did not understand in those days how the glory of 'man' is a huge obstacle to seeing the glory of 'God' in full manifestation and on a continual basis. Obadiah vs 3 says *The pride of your heart has deceived you...* Pride deceived and blinded me for many years and kept me from my destiny. I know for a fact I would be much further along in ministry today if I could have learned that lesson early on, about humility and the glory.

I believe it was God's grace that kept me from going very far in those days otherwise I would have fallen and that fall would have been devastating. I was not ready to handle a successful ministry. Your success can actually make you more susceptible to the fall, unless you know how to steward it all for His glory and His glory alone. Believe me. I have watched, just like my friend Pastor Steve Shank mentions in his book **God made Visible** in the chapter entitled '**The Domino Club**', many leaders who became success stories only to fall. Why? Because they could not address the pride and a byproduct of pride: deception that was in their heart, that led to their fall. They started out humble and being exalted but they did not remain in that place of humility and steward it for the Christ's glory. **Their success became their downfall.** Instead they became casualties along the way. Proverbs 16:18 says *Pride goes before destruction, And a haughty spirit before a fall.* When will the Body of Christ catch hold of this? How many more casualties will we have along the way?

In most Charismatic and Pentecostal circles we put a strong emphasis on the gifting of an individual, with a very low emphasis on Christlike character. Romans 11:29 says *For the gifts and the calling of God are irrevocable.* That is true. Today we see gifted people with great character flaws operating in the power of God and many Christians running after and hanging on every word they speak just because of the gifting of that individual. This is dangerous to the move of God. What we do is we put pressure on leaders to perform for their own glory, set them up for the fall, then we stand back and point the finger, wondering how they could fall.

What is more important to Jesus? Character (see Galatians 5:22-23) or gifting (see I Corinthians 12:7-10)? I would say if we looked at Jesus and the way He modeled this, character is more important. Character speaks of humility, intimacy, and relationship with the Father. Jesus had a strong emphasis on both, but more on character. We should put a strong emphasis on character, things like humility, integrity, honesty, love, patience, etc. At the same time put a strong emphasis on gifting also **but never let the gifting surpass the character.** This is the true test to see if we are ready for a lasting move of God where 'His glory' (not ours) will be manifested on the earth, through **continual** signs, wonders, miracles and healings.

Awhile back I read a Magazine where many key leaders wrote about the Glory of God coming to earth and that revival will break out. They wrote a lot about the grace of God. After reading many of the articles and skimming through the others I saw no mention of humility being tied to revival, the glory or grace. It was disappointing. Whatever good thing we have in life including signs, wonders, miracles comes by the grace of God. I do believe we need to understand and operate in God's grace. One of the best ways to see and experience the grace of God is by understanding and walking in humility. James 4:6 says *But He gives more grace. Therefore He says:* **"God resists the proud, But gives grace to the humble."** I Peter 5:5 says the same thing. James and Peter two key early church leaders later on in their life and ministry say almost word for word the same thing about pride and humility. Check it out James 4:6-10 & 1 Peter 5:5-9.

Both talk about drawing near to God. Who do you think He draws near to? Psalms 138:6 says *Though the Lord is on high, Yet* ***He regards the lowly; But the proud He knows from afar.*** James 4:6 says ***"God resists the proud."*** The word resists in the Greek means God ranges in battle against the proud. That is exactly where I was in the early days of ministry trying desperately to draw near to Him but feeling like I fell way short all the time. I wish I would of known He gives His grace to humble. I wish I had known He regards the lowly and humble but is so very far away from the proud and arrogant. Why does He regard and draw near to the humble? Because **He is humility in its purest form!**

Jesus invites us to partake of His very nature and what He is all about. He said *"Take* ***My yoke upon you*** *and* ***learn from Me,*** *for* ***I am gentle and lowly*** *in heart, and you will find rest for your souls. For My yoke is easy and My burden is light."* (Matthew 11:29-30). Ministry was difficult in those early days. I was constantly striving to make things take off for the ministry. If I would have taken Christ's yoke to learn of His humility my yoke would have been easy. The burden of ministry would have been light like it has become now wherever we travel to minister in this world.

How we Found our Destiny through Humility

During April 1998 we conducted a four day open air campaign in **Dandeli, Karnataka, India.** We saw about 9,500 people come to Christ, many wonderful miracles. Crowds grew up to about 7,000 during this outreach. I remember finishing this outreach being totally discouraged. I said to myself "I'm a failure. Look at my outreaches. We only had a crowd of 7,000 people show up for our outreach." I had been mentored by some great men of God who were winning millions of people to Christ worldwide. Some of their outreaches were reaching up to two hundred thousand people or more in a single service.

I was comparing myself with their ministry. The reason I was discouraged is because of my pride, arrogance and the image I was trying to live up to. 2 Corinthians 10:12 says *For we dare not class ourselves or compare ourselves with those who commend themselves. But they, measuring themselves by themselves, and comparing themselves among themselves, are not wise.* There is so much of this going on in the Body of Christ and all it does is breed strife and division. Comparing ourselves with others is all about the glory of man competing with the glory of God. It is not wise and in the long run it hinders the glory of God from being manifested on a continual basis.

Later in 1998 one of my board members Marc Gottfried

handed me a book entitled **The Final Quest** by Rick Joyner. Of any book I have read in my lifetime other than the Bible, I would have say this book had the most impact on my life and destiny when I allowed what was in it to transform my life and ministry for the better. This book talks about the pride and critical spirit in the Body of Christ in the last days. It was a real eye opener for Sharmila and I. We read this book a number of times and repented continually for the things we saw, that were wrong in our hearts in the area of pride. For the next 11 years I began to study about Christlike humility and pride before our book **Humility the Hidden Key to Walking in Signs and Wonders** was printed.

Back to 1998! When I started dealing with the pride and arrogance in my life, our ministry took a huge turn around. Later that year instead of looking where I could do a large open air campaign in India we choose to go to a remote unreached area in the foothills of the Himalaya Mountains where there were only about 90 believers in the entire city. We did a 4 day open air campaign in **Kashipur, Uttrakhand, India November 14-17, 1998.** The crowds never grew much larger than 3,000 people. Many were healed of blindness, deafness, paralysis and polio. Radical Hindu militants stormed our stage the 4th night and we were driven out of the city, unable to finish our outreach. Later after we left town Hindus beat up the radical

Hindu leader who shut down our outreach telling him *"you stopped a good thing."* As we left that city even though we could not finish the outreach we had great joy and peace knowing we were in God's perfect plan for our life. Around 2,200 came to Christ in this outreach.

As we traveled away from Kashipur we met a Hindu man who told us about this God named Jesus and what He had been doing in Kashipur. Newspapers in large cities far away from Kashipur reported about our outreach. Some good and some bad. Politicians came to our aid and said if we ever have any more trouble like this to let them know and they would stand with us.

In March 1-5, 2016 we returned to this city to complete what we started 18 years earlier. We saw another 3,600 come to Christ in this outreach. In this state there is only one Christian for every 300 people. Many powerful miracles took place. One night during this 2016 outreach Jesus appeared to many people during the praise and worship time performing mighty miracles and setting people free from demons. During this trip to Kashipur a 26 year old man came up to introduce himself to me. He attended our outreach in 1998 when he was eight years old. He said the miracles that Jesus did at that outreach so impacted his life that he accepted Jesus as Lord and Savior.

Now he is a pastor in Kashipur.

In the same state, in the outreach before Kashipur, October 6-10, 2015 both the former and present Chief Minister's sons came out to our event in total support of what we are doing. By humbling ourselves in 1998 Sharmila and I walked into our destiny. The blinders that were on our eyes fell and now we know who we are in Christ, His perfect will and know what we are really called to do. Pride kept me from fulfilling the call on my life but now Humility has helped me find out who Mark Anderson really is and what is my destiny. It is so fulfilling to be in this place, breaking open, impacting remote unreached areas in North India and Nepal for the sake of the Gospel of Jesus Christ. **To date in these two countries we have seen over 175,000 people come to Christ.** Most of them for the first time in their lives.

To find our destiny we need to follow the example of humility Jesus set for us. **Whatever He did he did for the 'Audience of One.'** He only did what He saw the Father doing. In Matthew 6:1-6 Jesus talks about the proper way to give and to pray. He said do not do these things to be seen by men but do them secretly and Father will reward you openly. When we learn to do things not for our own glory but for His only we are truly living for the 'Audience of One.' Let your motivation be only for His audience and not just to impress others. If you do this His glory will be manifested in your life to bring Him glory.

I have seen people over the years produce tremendous fruit after attending revival conferences in Toronto, Canada that changed their life. Like Heidi Baker. Since she attended the Toronto outpouring over 450 people have been raised from the dead in IRIS Ministries, millions of people have come into the Kingdom of God and many thousands of churches planted. On the other hand I have seen people attend the same conferences and come back and split churches and cause all kinds of problems and in the long run produce little or no fruit. What is the difference between the two that attended the same revival conferences? One went with humility and for the glory of God and other went in pride and arrogance, all for the glory of man. Which way will you go in life? Pursuing the glory of God or the glory of man? Humility and the glory go hand in hand. Let's pursue Jesus, His humility and watch His glory fall in our midst.

BOOKS ON THIS SUBJECT MATTER

If you would like more on this subject you can order Pastor Steve's book **God Made Visible, Seeing His Glory and Experiencing His Presence** from His website (www.stevecshank.com), Amazon Kindle or from www.markandersonministries.com/product/god-made-visible.

My book **Humility the Hidden Key to Walking in Signs and Wonders** is available through our website: www.markandersonministries.com/product/humility-the-hidden-key-to-walking-in-signs-and-wonders or through Amazon Kindle. It is available in German through Grain Press grain-press.jimdo.com/. In India, it is available in Hindi by contacting 0989707198.

Sundernagar, India outreach

Shalu had a miscarriage because her uterus was out of place. She felt an invisible hand move her uterus back into place.

Jyoti had to be carried to the meeting as she had been ill for months and could not walk. Her legs had turned blue. During mass prayer she was instantly energized by Holy Spirit and walked up and testified.

When our worship leader **Samarpan Sean** led us into an extended time of worship as everyone was worshipping, Mark asked if anyone had an encounter with Jesus or angels or was healed as result of that. Hands went up all over the crowd.

Sushma could barely speak and was shaking uncontrollably as she testified of seeing an angel whose head reached the top of the tent. She experienced severe heat and coolness after the angel touched her. She was instantly set free of the demons that were throwing her to the ground and making her cut herself the night before.

Ritika, a young girl had been praying for her mother who had stones in the kidneys and was scheduled for an operation. Ritika experienced extreme heat and began to speak in tongues and her mother felt the stones dissolve.

Mala Devi, a widow, was dying of breast cancer. She had come to Sundernagar to visit the temples, to try the appease the Hindu gods before she died. She wandered from one Hindu temple to another finding no peace. Someone invited her to the meeting. During worship she fell down. Then she felt an unseen hand lift her up. It was Jesus. She felt the oozing in her breasts stop. She said that now she has no fear of death as she knew she would be with Jesus.

We watched **Ranvir** shaking during worship. He testified that he saw a very handsome man in a white robe with longish hair on the stage smiling and waving to him. It was Jesus. Seeing Jesus waving at him, we asked Ranvir what did that make you feel like. He said he wanted to go hang out with Jesus.

Bimla - Saw Jesus in front of her wearing a crown. He placed His hand on her head and her body felt like boiling hot water & she was instantly healed of knee pain - **Sundarnagar,Himachal Pradesh, India June 7, 2013.**

Kashipur, India outreach

About 3,600 people turned to Christ in our 5 day outreach in
Kashipur, Uttarkhand, India March 1-5, 2016.

The young man on my right is 26 years old. When we ministered in Kashipur 18 years ago he gave his life Jesus at the age 8 years old as he was so impacted by the miracles Jesus did in those meetings. Today he is a Pastor in **Kashipur.**

Gurvinder Kaur - During extended worship time she spoke in tongues in English. Saw Jesus at a gate with His arms wide open. Jesus tells her to tell the people to open their hearts to Him to do great things - **Kashipur, India March 4, 2016.**

Sunita - Was tormented by demons for 15 years. Pastor Ankit had word of knowledge with her name and that Jesus was setting her free. Received freedom from demons- **Kashipur, UK, India March 2016.**

Ayush Kumar - born with bone blocking his nose. Healed and breathing through his nose for the 1st time in his life. One of our ministry team members Sylvi prayed over him - **Kashipur, India March 2, 2016.**

Anita - Weak and could not stand. Invisible hand helped her stand. Was very shy! Felt boldness to come and share before crowd - **Kashipur, India March 4, 2016.**

CHAPTER 7

Religion or Relationship? What Do You Have?

L et's look at Matthew 16: 5-7, 11-12 once again. *"Now when His disciples had come to the other side, they had forgotten to take bread. Then Jesus said to them, "Take heed and beware of the leaven of the Pharisees and the Sadducees." And they reasoned among themselves, saying, "It is because we have taken no bread." Jesus said ..."How is it you do not understand that I did not speak to you concerning bread?—but to beware of the leaven of the Pharisees and Sadducees." Then they understood that He did not tell them to beware of the leaven of bread, but of the doctrine of the Pharisees and Sadducees."* Notice in the verses above that Jesus tells his disciples, close followers *beware of the doctrine (or heart attitude) of the Pharisees and Sadducees.* He is saying beware of the religious spirit or spirit of **religion** (return

135

to bondage).

In the beginning of this book I mentioned in the Gospel accounts you could see by far the greatest opposition Jesus faced while walking this earth was from the religious leaders of His day or a religious spirit. It is no different today. The religious spirit progressed rapidly that after THESE LEADERS SAW HIM RAISE LAZARUS FROM THE DEAD (after fours days), in John 11, they wanted to kill him. Hard to believe after witnessing a miracle like that. In John 11:48 they said the reason for wanting to kill Him, *If we let Him alone like this, everyone will believe in Him...* A miracle working Jesus is unstoppable! But they had no interest in His glory but their only their own glory, fame and control. The biggest opposition to the Gospel (good news) today is a religious spirit or cold dead religion. This spirit desires to stop the living Christ and turn Him into something He's not; dead or lifeless. 2 Timothy 3:5 says in these last days many would be *having a form of godliness but denying its power. And from such people turn away.* We are instructed to literally run from dead or powerless religion.

There is a problem we have in the Body of Christ. Many are not taking Jesus words *'beware of the doctrine of the Pharisees and Sadducees'* seriously. They think we are charismatics or pentecostals so that does not pertain to us. Let's do some comparing between having religion versus having a living day to day relationship with Christ. As we look at these points allow Holy Spirit to convict us if we are not walking in a close relationship with the Living Christ. These are meant to build us up, encourage and help bring us into a closer walk with Jesus.

Religion or Relationship Test

#1- Do we use the Word of God to minister life or death? *There is one who speaks like the piercings of a sword, But the tongue of the wise promotes health* (Proverbs 12:18). The word of God is sharper than a two edged sword (see Hebrews 4:12). Something we all need to be mindful of is we can use the word of God to minister health and wholeness spirit, soul and body out of a relationship to Christ or use it to minister condemnation, guilt, heaviness, bondage, fear, etc out of a religious spirit. Many because of the effect of a religious spirit or religion use the word of God to hack people to pieces rather than ministering life. Jesus said *The thief does not come except to steal, and to kill, and to destroy. I have come that they may have life, and that they may have it more abundantly.* (see John 10:10). Religion is very much like a thief but our ultimate goal with God's word is to minister life.

#2- Do we have heart full of gratefulness and thanksgiving or are we complaining, critical and unthankful? Gratefulness and thanksgiving comes when we zero in and remember all

137

the good things God, by His grace has done and is doing in our lives. It sets up an atmosphere for faith and miracles to occur on a regular basis. Thanksgiving also turns to worship because our hearts are so full of praise, honor and the glory due Him.

Let me share something from our personal lives to bring home this point. Sharmila and I are constantly thanking God and giving glory to Him for what He has done and is doing in our lives. Two areas we continue thanking Him for is **divine health and divine protection.** At the time of writing this book I am only 58 years young. I am not able to give out Sharmila's age or I will face the wrath of Sharmila. Not a good thing! We are not that young. Apart from our daughter Charisma's birth we have never had medical insurance in our lifetime. Nor have we needed it. Now before I go any further we are not against medical insurance. We are not telling people to go without medical insurance. If we felt led we were to get medical insurance we would get it. At this time we do not need it.

We do our part in the natural realm. We are given to exercise, nutrition, proper rest, and care of our physical bodies, even in the midst a busy travel schedule overseas of about six times a year. We constantly thank God for guiding us in this area of our lives. We constantly thank Him for Jesseca Cross, the lady who owns the gym we work out in, in Cody, Wyoming where we live. She was a US Olympian and was also inducted into the University of Wyoming Hall of Fame. She has given so much insight to Sharmila which in turn keeps us walking in health. Sharmila has tremendous knowledge of what to eat and what not to eat to stay healthy. We are constantly thanking Him for this knowledge. You might think that is something so small. That is where believers miss it. It's all about a heart overwhelmed with thanksgiving to Him for His goodness. It creates an atmosphere for the miraculous.

We hardly know what it is like to be sick. We have not had a disease and have not been hospitalized (apart from our daughter's birth) because of the goodness and grace of our great God. Have we been sick or injured? Yes! Not often though. We also have been supernaturally healed by Holy Spirit a number of times. Most of the time, not immediately, but over a period of time, supernaturally. If it was not for His intervention in healing us, in a couple cases we would have been in the hospital, needing surgery. In our entire lifetime our dental and medical bills have been very, very low. For this also we give our Lord, Savior, Healer and Protector Jesus Christ all the praise, glory and honor. What happens in return as we do this? We continue to experience His glory in the area of health, well being and divine protection.

I am so grateful I can still play basketball and football. I can go to our High School football field and kick long Field Goals like I did when I was young because the Lord healed my knee. www.markandersonministries.com/category/videos/page/3 See **Mark's personal testimony of knee healing.** I am so grateful when I have time to go hunting and camping (on foot) in our lovely Wyoming mountains. I can still jog even though I am extremely slow compared to Sharmila and my daughter Charisma. I am continually thanking Him for being healthy enough to still do these things. Only He has made this possible and I give Him all the glory and honor from a very thankful heart. What happens as I give Him all that glory for this? I continue walking in divine health. He is a good God and He is so good to Sharmila and I.

We travel all over the world knowing we are in His perfect will. Being in His perfect will is a place of safety. We know what it is like to have Psalm 91 operating in our lives. Psalm 34:7-8 says *The angel of the Lord encamps all around those who fear Him, And delivers them. Oh, taste and see that the Lord is good; Blessed is the man who trusts in Him!* We have had a couple close calls as far as danger goes but always been supernaturally protected by Holy Spirit and angels. We constantly tell others of His goodness to us in the area of our health and protection. Year after year, after year, the same thing. Divine health, well being and protection! Can having a thankful heart have anything to do with that? You bet it does!

Now these are just two areas we are so thankful. I could make a long list of His goodness to us. When we have time at home we like to have a night of no agenda worship, to worship Him and also just to thank Him for all He has done for us and is continuing to do for us.

He shows personal favoritism to no man or woman (see Galatians 2:6). We are not special. His Word, grace and favor work in our lives as we give Him the glory, honor and praise for these things, and it can do the same for you.

Psalm 78:41-42 says *Yes, again and again* **they tempted God,** *and* **limited the Holy One of Israel.** *They* **did not remember His power:** *The day when He redeemed them from the enemy.* Complaining, unthankfulness, and the critical spirit creates an atmosphere of unbelief where miracles, the blessings and healing rarely occur. If we fall to this religious spirit we actually tempt God and limit His power. It also can be open doors to bringing curses in our lives. When we forget his miracles and blessings in our life we forget His power and unbelief is the byproduct.

If you look at Deuteronomy 28 it talks about the blessings (1- 14) and curses (15-68) of not following the law. If you look at the curse of the law it basically says anything that can go wrong will go wrong. Verse 47-48 shows the heart of what religion and breaking the law can do. *Because you **did not serve** the Lord your God with **joy and gladness of heart,** for the abundance of everything, therefore you shall serve your enemies...* When we follow religion, the law, add unthankfulness and complaining to it, it leads to all kinds of problems, just like Israel experienced (see 1 Corinthians 10:10-12). All said and done in relationship with Christ we are free to be thankful because *Christ has redeemed us from the curse of the law, having become a curse for us...* (Galatians 3:13).

#3- Is your walk based on your good works or His grace? Many try working up the blessings and promises of God not understanding that all the blessings, signs, wonders, miracles, healings, etc come by the grace of God. You can not work them up. Notice what the Apostle Paul said in 1 Corinthians 15:10 *But by the grace of God I am what I am, and His grace toward me was not in vain; but **I labored more abundantly than they all,** yet not **I, but the grace of God which was with me.*** Are we catching what Paul says here? Paul worked harder than anyone else but it was not him but the grace of God that helped him do that. Grace is not an excuse to become lazy and passive. It is an enabler that allows us to do more than we could ever imagine doing. The work and favor we have in India along with the harvest we are

142

seeing seems to be greatly accelerating way beyond anything we could ever achieve in our own strengh. We have learned things that have helped us tap into the grace of God, to help us go to a whole new level in ministry and accomplish so much more than we ever thought possible.

#4- Is your revelation of God based mostly on the Old Testament or the New Testament? Before Calvary or after Calvary? Many believers in Christ live their lives as if Christ never went to Calvary. From what side of the cross are you living your life? In Christian circles many times you can tell which side of Calvary people are living their lives from. Just see what they are experiencing in life and what is coming out of their mouths. In many circles more sermons are preached on things from the Old Testament but very few messages from the New. Don't get me wrong. I use and study both Old and New Testament verses. But my revelation of verses in the Old Testament are in light of what was accomplished at Calvary.

Why should I settle for the **double portion of Elijah's spirit (mantle)** when **Jesus had the Spirit without measure and said I could have the same.** For me perfect theology is found in Jesus Christ. You can not find much better theology than what Jesus had. Most of the revelation I want is of Jesus Christ and what He accomplished at Calvary. Paul said in

Colossians 1:26-27 *the mystery which has been* **hidden from ages and from generations,** *but now has been revealed to His saints. To them God willed to make known what are the riches of the* **glory of this mystery** *among the Gentiles: which is* **Christ in you, the hope of glory.** A great mystery was hid for many generations until Christ went to Calvary defeated sin, Satan, demons, sickness and gave us a New Covenant with His shed blood. No longer do I have live with a revelation of the Old Testament (Covenant) but I can live my life on the other side of Calvary or in the New Testament (Covenant). What does that look like? Now God the Creator is living His life through me on this earth (see Colossians 2:9-10). I can live from from a whole different realm. I can rise up to His realm (Zoe Life- The very life of God).

#5- No hunger, no change! Jesus said in Matthew 5:6 *Blessed are those who hunger and thirst for righteousness, For they shall be filled.* If there is no hunger for spiritual things in your life eventually you will starve spiritually. If I am hungry for something in the natural like a Big Mac and happen to go by a McDonalds there is a very good chance I will be filled with a Big Mac. If we hunger for His presence we will be filled with His presence. If we hunger to learn of healing we begin to study and look for healing. Eventually we will be filled and partaking of healing. That is how God's natural and spiritual laws work. You become filled with what you hunger for. The religious leaders of Jesus day had no hunger and therefore no change took place in their life for the better.

#6- One can have a religious passion or a passion birthed out relationship. As a young preacher I was passionate for Christ and to win the lost. As a result I was constantly leading people to Christ one on one. After awhile of teaching and training others for soul winning I began to become very critical and judgmental of many believers because they were not winning the lost like I was. Soon the anointing on my life to win the lost one on one began to diminish or burn out. How many other followers of Christ allow their passion for Him to turn into a critical spirit and eventually burn out? I can imagine some of the religious leaders of Jesus day started out with a passion to serve God but became critical of everyone and became stagnant with their walk. What is sad, many of them missed out on the Messiah Jesus being in their midst.

Jesus said to the religious leaders in John 5:39-40 *You search the Scriptures, for in them you think you have eternal life; and these are they which testify of Me. But you are not willing to come to Me that you may have life.* The critical spirit and arrogance blinded them to eternal life and a relationship with God Creator, who was mentioned time and time in the very scriptures they studied religiously. A religious spirit kept them bound and blinded from the truth, standing right in front of them. There are 70 major prophecies of the Messiah in the Old Testament (over 300 total). Jesus fulfilled them all. Yet these religious leaders who studied those scriptures day after day did not believe he was the Messiah. Why? Because their religious spirit, arrogance, and critical spirit hindered them from seeing Him as the Messiah. They figured they knew better than Father God what the Messiah would be like. Jesus did not fit into their religious box.

#7- Are you walking in love or doom and gloom? Psalm 145:8-9 says *The Lord is gracious and full of compassion, Slow to anger and great in mercy. The Lord is good to all...* There are many Christians who teach solely or gravitate towards the anger and judgment of God. Their concept of God is that He is always angry. They carry a spirit of heaviness and gloom many because of their distorted view of the God the Father, maybe because of experiences in life with their own earthly father. Whenever something looks bleak they come along and quickly prophecy judgment, doom and gloom. Let me expound further on this.

How are we to act to the contrary? The word Gospel means good news! News is something that already took place. What Jesus did 2,000 years ago and still doing today is GOOD NEWS (THE GOSPEL). This is what the world needs. We do have doom and gloom all over the world but what is our focus to be as followers of Jesus Christ? It is to spread the good news of Jesus Christ. Jesus even foretold of this time in history in Luke 21:26 in the Amplified *people fainting from fear and expectation of the [dreadful] things coming on the world; for the [very] powers of the heavens will be shaken.* Are we to live in fear and heaviness, and with all the health problems associated with that? No! Jesus defeated Satan and overcame this world and now He lives in us.

Paul said in Romans 1:15-16 Amplified says *So, for my part, I am **ready and eager to preach the gospel** also to you who are in Rome. I am **not ashamed of the gospel,** for it is the **power of God for salvation** [from His wrath and punishment] to everyone who believes [in Christ as Savior]...* Paul's focus was not all the bad things happening in the world or to him but his focus was the good news because it brought power. Power for what? **Salvation!** The word salvation means to have our sins forgiven, eternal life, bodily healing, deliverance, protection and so much more. What does that mean? That means if I am focused on the Good News of Jesus Christ I will be a carrier of salvation, healing, protection, deliverance, and forgiveness to the world and for myself.

Romans 2:4 says *Or do you despise the riches of His goodness, forbearance, and longsuffering, not knowing that the **goodness*** *of God leads you to repentance?* This was the Apostle Paul's message: The good news of Jesus Christ! It is in sharing and demonstrating the good news of Jesus Christ that will turn our nation and world to Jesus, not focusing in on all the negatives. If followers of Jesus spread fear and heaviness and veer from the Gospel message, then our country could very well spiral downward. If we offer no hope to the hopeless, His power will be quenched by a religious spirit. The greatest opposition to the Gospel does not come from the lost, it comes from this religious spirit within the church, same as in Jesus' day.

#8- The glory of man versus the GLORY OF GOD. Which one will triumph in your life? How many moves of God have been shut down because of the glory of man coming on the scene? This is not about us and our great talents. This is all about Jesus and the lost souls He came to die for. In Isaiah 42:8 God says *My glory I will not give to another.* Jesus is willing to allow His glory to fill us and consume us in order for heaven to literally invade this earth. Our only requirement is we have to keep the glory of man from stealing the show and know how to rightfully handle His glory in our life.

Isaiah 60:1-3 says *Arise, shine; For your light has come! And the **glory of the Lord is risen upon you.** For behold, the **darkness shall cover the earth,** And **deep darkness the people; But the**

Lord will arise over you, And His glory will be seen upon you. The Gentiles shall come to your light, And kings to the brightness of your rising. Darkness will cover the people of this earth. What is our reaction to that doom and gloom? **BUT the Lord will arise over you, And His glory will be seen upon you.** That is what the good news of Jesus Christ is all about. He is doing more miracles, healing, signs, wonders, showing favor in this earth than any other time in history. So let's be good stewards of His glory. If we can be, then His glory will increase in our lives more and more. In my closing point I will share how to carry His glory with the right attitude so 'the (His) glory' can increase in your life.

#9- *Nevertheless even among the rulers many believed in Him, but because of the Pharisees they did not confess Him, lest they should be put out of the synagogue; for* **they loved the praise of men more than the praise of God** (John 12:42-43). Loving the praises of men more than the praises of God is a sure way to terminate the move of God or glory of God down. Move after move have been terminated because **men and women went from pursuing the glory of God coming down to loving the praises of men more than the praises or glory of God.**

Jesus said in Matthew 6:1-6 *"Take heed that you do not do your charitable deeds* **before men, to be seen by them. Otherwise** *you have no reward from your Father in heaven. Therefore, when you do a charitable deed, do not sound a trumpet before you as the hypocrites do in the synagogues and in the streets, that they may have glory from men. Assuredly, I say to you, they have their reward. But when you do a charitable deed, do not let your left hand know what your right hand is doing, that your charitable deed may be in secret; and your Father who sees in secret will Himself reward you openly. "And when you pray, you shall not be like the hypocrites. For they love to pray standing in the synagogues and on the corners of the streets, that they may be seen by men. Assuredly, I say to you, they have their reward. But you, when you pray, go into your room, and when you have shut your door, pray to your Father who is in the secret place; and your Father who sees in secret will reward you openly.* This is one point we have hammered home hard to workers in India and Nepal and the reason we are seeing such a great move of God in Northern India and parts of Nepal. Are we living our lives to be seen and glorified by men or are we living our lives for THE AUDIENCE OF ONE? This makes all the difference whether we will see a lasting move of God that impacts eternity or we just waste precious time on this earth. Do you want to impact eternity for His glory? Then live your life, from relationship for HIS AUDIENCE ONLY! Nothing in this world can compare to seeing His glory invade this earth and living for **His audience only.**

CHAPTER 8

The Person of the Holy Spirit

Continuing on with the theme of religion versus relationship another area of concern is intimacy with Holy Spirit. Are we longing to hear His voice and follow His direction for our life. Bono the lead singer of the rock band U2 says about Holy Spirit, *"I often wonder if religion is the enemy of God. It's almost like religion is what happens when the Spirit has left the building."* Without Holy Spirit all we have is dead religion. Apostle Paul warned us of this danger in the last days. *Holding to a form of [outward] godliness (religion), although they have denied its power [for their conduct nullifies their claim of faith]. Avoid such people and keep far away from them* (2 Timothy 3:5 Amp). We are to flee dead religion and those who promote it.

Jesus talking about Holy Spirit said this in John 16:7-16. *"Nevertheless I tell you the truth. It is to your advantage* (Greek - **profitable, expedient**) *that I go away; for if I do not go away, the Helper will not come to you; but if I depart, I will send Him to you. And when He has come, He will convict* (Greek - also means **convince**) *the world of sin, and of righteousness, and of judgment: of sin, because they do not believe in Me; of righteousness, because I go to My Father and you see Me no more; of judgment, because the ruler of this world is judged. "I still have many things to say to you, but you cannot bear them now. However, when He, the Spirit of truth, has come, He will guide you into all truth; for He will not speak on His own authority, but whatever He hears He will speak; and He will tell you things to come. He will glorify Me, for He will take of what is Mine and declare it to you. All things that the Father has are Mine. Therefore I said that He will take of Mine and declare* (Greek- declare, reveal, transmit) *it to you "A little while, and you will not see Me; and again a little while, and you will see Me, because I go to the Father."*

In verse 13-15 Jesus is constantly referring to Holy Spirit as "He". In these verses, He refers to Holy Spirit as "He" ten times. I think in doing so Jesus is establishing a fact. Holy Spirit is a person, an integral part of the Trinity and worthy of worship and relationship. Holy Spirit is not some kind of an unseen presence or an impersonal wind that blows in and out. Holy

Spirit longs for us to be intimate with Him so He can reveal, declare and transmit to our spirit man things pertaining to our future.

In the early 1980s I was working as a carpenter in Aspen, Colorado on a large townhouse building. I was looking for opportunities to share Christ with my co-workers with little success. Finally one day at lunch one of the workers asked if I wanted to go get high on some weed and drunk with the rest of the crew after work. I told him I did not need that because Jesus gives me a great high. He told me don't tell me about your Jesus. Little did he know the Bible calls our God 'The Most High.' I would rather get high on 'The Most High' than some substitute or counterfeit.

Even though this guy did not want to hear anything about Jesus he started going around the job site telling everyone about the Jesus fanatic at work. With his help I ended up taking five guys to church one night for a midweek service. Three of them spoke Spanish and did not understand the preaching but the other two were Americans. The American men really enjoyed the service. I asked one man, Noah if he wanted to accept Christ that night. He told me "not now" but that he was interested in going to the church again. I told him I could take him on Sunday.

Later that week we worked together and were scheduled for overtime on Saturday but he never showed up to work. Later that night about 3:30am Holy Spirit woke me up. I waited on Him to find out what was happening. He transmitted to my spirit man, 'bind the spirit of suicide.' I took authority and bound that spirit and then prayed in tongues, allowing Holy Spirit to pray through me. Finally after praying for awhile I had peace and went back to sleep.

The next morning I went to pick up Noah for church service. He stayed in a place where many of the workers from out of town stayed. I went in and nobody was around. So I began leaving. As I passed by a bedroom door I heard a faint sound from inside the room and felt like I needed to open it. I was not prepared for what I saw. Blood was all over the room. An empty bottle of sleeping pills on the dresser. That did not work. Then Noah cut his wrist that did not work. Finally he cut his main artery and blood was all over the room. He was laying in a puddle of his own blood. The only thing that kept him from bleeding to death was his arm was folded and blood began to dry.

I called for the ambulance and called the church to pray. Noah was put in intensive care. I asked my Pastor, Bruce Porter to visit him the next day because I had to be at work. Pastor

Bruce went to hospital where Noah was awake and recovering. He found out that everything that could go wrong for Noah went wrong. Noah's wife left him. Someone stole his luggage and nothing good was happening. He decided to take his life. Pastor Bruce shared the good news of Jesus with Noah, he received Christ as Lord and like a lightbulb something went on in the inside. All of sudden he had a reason to live. We traveled to Minnesota together. I counseled him a bit in his walk with Christ before parting ways.

I thank Holy Spirit for leading me to evangelize at work even though the response was not good at first. I thank Him for transmitting to my spirit man to bind the spirit of suicide and pray in the tongues for Noah. If I had not been obedient to my partner, Holy Spirit, Noah would be in hell today without Christ. We need Holy Spirit to transmit to our spirit man things that pertain to the future.

Jesus tells us that when Holy Sprit comes things will get much better. Better than when He was walking this earth in the flesh. One thing Holy Spirit will bring is conviction of sin, to show people their need for a Savior. Many years ago I learned this while doing street evangelism in downtown Minneapolis. My friend Joe and I were winding up the night in sharing on the streets when I noticed a guy across the street (drug addict) and felt we needed to go talk with him. On my way over to to him I was thinking what I could say when I approached him. Once I got up to him I said *"did you know Jesus loves you?"* That is all the further I got as Holy Spirit was already convicting him. He cried out *"I want to get saved."* I thought but I have not given him the plan of salvation yet or quoted any scriptures. I did not need to. He prayed right then and there to make Jesus the Lord of his life.

Either someone had warned him that I was a long winded preacher and if he just accepted Jesus I would not preach to him or Holy Spirit showed up before I ever arrived and showed this drug addict his need for Savior. I tend to think it was the latter.

Think about Moses and Israelites. They had an opportunity to get real close and intimate with the Creator of the universe but instead they told Moses to do it for them and look where it led them. *Now all the people witnessed the thunderings, the lightning flashes, the sound of the trumpet, and the mountain smoking; and when the people saw it, they trembled and **stood afar off.** Then they said to Moses, "You speak with us, and we will hear; but **let not God speak with us,** lest we die." ... So the **people stood afar off,** but **Moses drew near** the thick darkness where God was.* (Exodus 20:18-19, 21). Moses cried out Show me your glory (Exodus 33:18). He was able to see the glory of God and talk with God on a regular basis because His heart was for relationship and intimacy rather than religion.

Do you long to hear His voice? This is where I have struggled in recent years. I get real busy with ministry, praying, asking God, interceding but very little time waiting on my partner Holy Spirit. I am believing for change here. Even more so as I see what is taking place around this world. I need to get still before Him and train my spirit to hear His voice better, more often and allow Him to transmit to my spirit man things that pertain to the future.

Be still, and know that I am God; *I will be exalted among the nations, I will be exalted in the earth* (Psalm 46:10)! Think about this invitation be still before Him, know Him intimately, wait on Him and He will be exalted in the nations. Is not that the goal we have in mind when it comes to ministry to see Him high and lifted up with multitudes flocking to Him. We need to become carriers of His presence or like Bono said, Holy Spirt has left the building. What a waste of precious God-given time if He leaves the building. Then all we have is religion and striving to get things done. It looks good and religious on the outside but it's not of God!

Once my wife Sharmila, a tough woman who loves weightlifting slipped on ice and fell in the hills behind our home while walking our dog. She was in a lot of pain. At times it brought her to tears. We prayed at times when the pain was intense and she would get some temporary relief but the injury still caused a lot of pain. A short time later we were in Redding, California in January to get ordained and licensed by Randy Clark and Bill Johnson. Randy introduced both of us to Bill and he shook our hands. When he shook Sharmila's hand something happened. As soon as he left she said *"My back is on fire."* So I felt her back. Sure enough it was on fire and soaked in sweat (in January). Later that afternoon we were listening to Randy Clark teaching at the conference when Sharmila said by the way my back does not hurt anymore. She was completely healed just by a simple anointed handshake.

We need to get to know Holy Spirit in an intimate way so we can be carriers of His presence, just like Pastor Bill was when Sharmila needed a miracle. People are dependent on us being carriers of His presence. Be still, and we will know Him intimately and become carriers of His presence.

Isaiah 40:31 says *But those who **wait*** (Hebrew- to become one with, entwined) *on the Lord Shall **renew*** (Hebrew- change, alter) *their strength; They shall mount up with wings like eagles, They shall run and not be weary, They shall walk and not faint.* When we wait upon Holy Spirit we literally become one with

Him or entwined so intimately we flow in perfect union with Him and Jesus' plan for our lives. It will cause us to change from doing things in our natural strength to supernatural strength to accomplish whatever He sets before us to do. His grace kicks in and no matter whatever the task there is no weariness or burnout.

Notice this verse says we *mount up with wings like eagles.* The neat thing about eagles is that it can be storming and tumultuous but they just lock their wings and soar way above the storm clouds and bask in the sun, way above life's troubles. They have a bird's eye view of the 'little' problems below. The same happens to us when we wait on Holy Spirit. We soar above life's problems and have a Word's eye view of the little problems below us. All the while basking in the SON.

Romans 10:17 says *So then faith comes by hearing, and hearing by the word of God.* The word word here is the Greek word Rhema. It means the spoken word of God. Faith does not come by reading the word. It helps! But unless that word comes alive in your spirit by it becoming the spoken word to your given situation there is little or no active or activated faith. When God speaks a word from heaven to your given circumstances, come hell or high water that word will be fulfilled. All you have to do is act on that word. There is enough faith and enough power in every spoken or rhema word from heaven. All we have to do is act on that word.

A perfect example of this is Peter walking on the water. *So He (Jesus) said, "**Come.**" And when Peter had come down out of the boat, he walked on the water to go to Jesus.* How was He able to walk on water? There was enough faith and **enough power behind that one word COME spoken by Jesus,** that all Peter had to do was act on that word and he could defy the laws of gravity. Peter walked on the water but as soon as He took his eye off Jesus (the Living Word of God) and looked at the wind and waves (circumstances) he began to sink.

Communion of the Holy Spirit

The grace of the Lord Jesus Christ, and the love of God, and the communion of the Holy Spirit be with you all. Amen (2 Corinthians 13:14). The Greek word for **communion** is *Koinonia*; it also means **fellowship and partnership.** All three of these things are so vital if you want to have a living relationship with Holy Spirt and not just religion.

COMMUNION - In simple English this word implies communicating or talking with someone. It is imperative to understand that communion is two ways. That entails talking and **listening.** James 1:19 says, *"… let every man be swift to hear slow to speak… "* In our relationship with the Holy Spirit not only should we spend time communicating or talking with Him, but also spend a lot of time **listening to what He has to say.**

Early in ministry I learned about communion the hard way. Once while witnessing in Forest Lake, Minnesota I saw a man eating in a McDonalds Restaurant. I figured I would go share with him. I started preaching to him. Five minutes into my nice message (so I thought) he interrupts me and says *"Hey buddy, conversation is two ways."* I never did get another word in. He started telling me about the cult he belonged to and because he had listened to me I had to return the favor. I learned the hard way *be swift to hear, slow to speak.*

FELLOWSHIP - relates to the time we spend with our friends, getting to know them and enjoying their company. Proverbs 18:24, *"A man who has friends must himself be friendly, But there is a friend who sticks closer than a brother."* I believe Holy Spirit desires to be a friend who will stick closer to us than a brother. If we spend time with Holy Spirit, fellowshipping with Him, then His voice will become very clear, one that we will be able to recognize easily. I can recognize my wife's voice in a big crowd, even if I do not see her. Why? Because I communicate with her, listen to her and have fellowship with her.

By listening to Holy Spirit we are more effective and

successful in ministry, and in every decision we make in life. He always speaks wisdom and gives explicit guidance for every situation in life. All we have to do is wait and listen. By fellowshipping with Holy Spirit we will be able to recognize His voice. Hearing God speak is not that difficult. All it takes is an intimate relationship with Him.

PARTNERSHIP - usually refers to two or more people working together toward a common goal. These people make decisions together, work together and meet often to discuss progress towards the given goal. Holy Spirit desires to enter into a similar arrangement with us, if we are willing. Every morning we need to acknowledge Holy Spirit and ask Him what He wants to do through us and then be obedient to follow through with what He speaks.

These three aspects are the keys to a successful relationship with Holy Spirit. Many in the healing ministry will place a strong emphasis on the word and faith, which is good; but to only have that without knowing Holy Spirit intimately is like having the power in you without an outlet for expressing it. It also leads to an imbalance in one's life.

Kathryn Kulhman was one of the prominent ministers who placed a great emphasis on the person and partnership of Holy Spirit. Kathryn Kulhman enjoyed an extremely intimate relationship with Holy Spirit. Her life and ministry are a testimony of how an intimate relationship with Holy Spirit can radically change one's life. In the middle of her large outreaches she would hold conversations with Holy Sprit, oblivious to the thousands of people around her. As Holy Spirit would speak to her He would tell her conditions He wanted to heal. She would call out those conditions. Many hopeless cripples would jump out of wheelchairs. Terminally ill people would be instantly healed. Powerful, undeniable miracles flowed freely in her meetings. She was an example of someone who understood partnership, fellowship and communion with Holy Spirit.

Sukhar, Nepal Outreach

Mangri - 101 years old was suffering with asthma and pain in his chest for 35 years. Instantly healed by Jesus!

Bandia Devi - blind from cataracts for 5 years. Healed by Christ!

Krisha - 26 years old! Had tumor on neck for 8 years. Was ozzing! Instantly dissolves. No sign of tumor!

16 years old! Was totally blind and eyes were bugging out. Able to start seeing now after Jesus heals her eyes!

Sukhar, Nepal Outreach

Sita Ram - Deaf for seven years! Healed by Jesus!

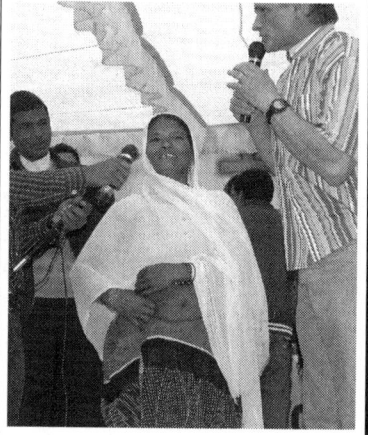

Ram Devi - One of many healed of kidney stones. Suffered for 4 years!

Rashu - Was blind for 3 or 4 years. Instantly healed by Christ!

Introducing pastors to the audience and encouraging new believers to go to their church.

Young boy whose arm was severely crippled and bent shows how Jesus healed him.

Praying over pastors before sending them out into crowd to pray for the sick.

Bandi Kumari - 78 years old, bent over for last 12 years! Now back has straightened out after a pastor prayed over her.

About 3,800 attend last day of Sukhar, Nepal outreach. Around 4,300 came to Christ during this 3-day outreach.

Antram - 90 years old paralyzed on left side. Came to stage laughing showing how Jesus healed him and he can lift his left arm now.

Arun Chaudhary - 12 years old could not see for 5 years. Prayed for by pastor now can see clearly!

Leadership conference in Sukhar, Nepal. Many had powerful encounters with Holy Spirit during prayer for baptism of the Holy Spirit and impartation time.

CHAPTER 9

The Motivating Force of Purpose & Vision

Once we begin to enter into intimacy and start hearing the voice of Holy Spirit, then we need to allow Him to fill our life with God given purpose, vision and goals. This is when we will begin to greatly impact this world and our sphere of influence. *"Without vision the people perish..."* Proverbs 29:18 What motivates us in life? Or do we lack motivation? God desires us to be people of vision and purpose. Without vision and purpose we stagnate, wasting precious God given time and multitudes perish around us.

Deuteronomy chapter 2 is a classic example of people without vision. It chronicles the story of the Israelites meanderings, making no headway towards the Promised Land. God said, *"You have compassed this mountain long enough, turn you northward"* (Duet. 2:3). Do you feel like the Israelites on occasions? Many of us have spent years roaming the mountains, spinning our wheels going nowhere. Every child of God is full of potential. We tap into that potential with a clear cut vision and purpose in life. If we have vision and purpose in life we will not wander aimlessly through the mountains, rather we will conquer the mountains in our lives as God has willed for each of us. This works in all areas of life.

Much of America has gotten sidetracked from and lost its vision and purpose in recent years. It has resulted in electing leaders without considering future consequences. Proverbs 28:16 says *A ruler who lacks understanding is a great oppressor.* When Heads of nations lack understanding of the Creator of the universe and His purpose for their lives they become oppressors of their people. They keep their people from rising up with vision, purpose and goals. This is how nations are "dumbed down" and begin to gradually spiral downwards. The people have no vision or purpose for the future. They are just living for the here and now, letting government decide the future for them. I have been to many former Communist countries and still see this affect on those nations today. A poverty mindset and apathy are a big part of their lives, even many years after communism.

The Effects of a Positive Vision

Vision and purpose will wake us up each day and set us in a specific direction. It fills our life with peace, joy and godly contentment. Lack of vision or purpose can lead us towards laziness, stagnation, insecurity, procrastination, apathy, and discouragement.

When I graduated from high school in 1976 I only had one purpose in my life. That was to play football (American style football) at Normandale Junior College, in Bloomington, Minnesota. It was a college that usually placed towards the top in the nation in junior college football. I was not a gifted athlete like my father was in high school. To be honest with you I do not have the natural talent for most of the things I have done in life and am still doing.

I played high school football at a small town school. I was a Kicker, 6'2" and 145 lbs. That does not enable you to do a whole lot in tackle football. I was the first kicker in my high school's history to attempt field goals and kick extra points. I had a good senior year in football and wanted to play college football. When my friends heard I wanted to play for Normandale Junior College, they thought it was a joke. To be honest with you unless I greatly improved it was a joke.

Once I decided to play college football I began to get

extremely focused. I had a purpose, goal and a vision before me to motivate myself. I wanted to make that football team. Nothing would get in my way. I begin to lift weights consistently and began eating a lot more. I practiced kickoffs and field goals daily. I ran regularly. I would be out kicking and running even in lightening and thunderstorms, disregarding weather warnings. I remember running in a downpour. I saw lightning hit close behind me and also hit close in front of me. Call it stupidity and foolishness! I did not care. I was totally focused on my goal. Thank God for His grace in protecting me in those days!

Come the Fall of 1977 I made the team. I weighed 165 lbs. I was in great shape. I made the final cut and was on the travel squad. I played kicker behind an All American Kicker, who led the nation in scoring, for junior colleges. To keep him free from injuries many times I was called upon to do the kickoffs. My kickoff average increased by 10 yards per kick from my Senior year in high school. In the last game of the season, on my last kickoff I almost put the kick through the end zone. In that game I also had the chance to play 3rd string wide receiver and caught a pass for 1st down. Some of my high school buddies were at the game and were in shock.

How did I make this team? I had a vision and purpose! It woke me up in the mornings and motivated me to get somewhere in life. The next year I was considering going out for the football team again. However, I became greatly sidetracked from that vision to something much different. I practiced with the team before the season started. I ended up spending more time witnessing and sharing my faith that year than practicing. When school started I decided to pursue something else in life. I had been baptized in Holy Spirit in the Spring of 1978 and was launched into world evangelism. I met some of my teammates later in life. Turns out I was able to have a great impact on their life in helping them come into a relationship with Christ. I used that lesson from the motivating force of purpose to get where I am today in worldwide ministry.

This teaching can help a person in all areas of life, both in the natural and spiritual realms. Whether it is in ministry, sports, politics, marriage, missions, business, or media. If one allows Holy Spirit inspired purpose to be birthed in one's life it will motivate us and bring success to all areas of our lives. This is part of living an abundant and fulfilling life.

When we are filled with vision people will gravitate towards us which results in a team working together for the fulfillment of a specific goal. United or corporate action is very effective. When something good becomes our passion, coupled with vision and purpose, one has tapped into success in this life.

Without consistent vision and purpose we tend to live off yesterday's accomplishments and have nothing fresh from heaven to offer people today. Vision and purpose should be an integral part of our lives if we desire to accomplish our goals. Do not live off yesterday's victories. New battles rage today!

There is a battle raging for the soul of this nation. While believers in Christ have sat back the ungodly, like Billionaire **George Soros, an athiest who loves playing God (do a web search for 'Puppet Master')** have had clear vision, purpose, have strategized and planned well, especially regarding America's destiny and how to take her down. George Soros has figured out how to take control of the media, education, politics, arts and entertainment, etc. Much of the 2016 chaos and violent rioting in the USA was and is funded by George Soros and his organizations. He has funded and paid people who have no vision and purpose in life other than to riot and cause extreme chaos in the USA. His clear cut purpose is to get Hillary Clinton in as President in 2016.

We can clearly see much of the USA media is extremely biased regarding the 2016 election like no other time in history. You can clearly see today how the media is bought and paid for by America haters, the God haters and immoral. It is apparent in the media's silence on so many critical issues that we need investigation and answers. They will only report their bias and do their best to take America off course, distracted by what is not important like they have for many years now. They have purpose, goals and many of these media outlets are funded by George Soros. We need to look into this and do our homework. They have a purpose and that is to remove God from America. We need believers with clear cut vision and purpose to take back and conquer these spheres of influence in society.

You can Know your Future

As Christians can we know our future? Many think this is not possible. Some will quote Matthew 6:34 (KJV), **Take therefore no thought for the morrow:** *for the morrow shall take thought for the things of itself. Sufficient unto the day is the evil thereof.* They say we do not need to think about or plan for tomorrow, rather live 'one day at a time sweet Jesus' (popular old Christian song). This verse when studied in the original Greek and interpreted in the correct context is actually encouraging us not to be anxious or worry about tomorrow. Worrying about tomorrow will actually prevent us from doing what God wants us to do today. Fear is very destructive. Jesus speaking of the last days said men's **hearts failing them from fear and the expectation** *of those things which are coming on the earth, for the powers of the heavens will be shaken* (Luke 21:26).

Health problems are brought on by giving into fear and having a negative outlook on life.

We need to rise up with humility, boldness and courage like George Washington and our early founders did when they faced impossible odds. We need to quit living in fear, with the 'one day at a time sweet Jesus' mindset, get a vision and purpose nailed down to take this country back. Much of this passive lifestyle comes from the influence of Greek Philosophy and also Calvinism in Western Christianity. Greek philosophy teaches us to just focus on the spiritual and forget the natural realm. Calvinism brings about a 'whatever will be will be' attitude, which keeps a lot of Christians from pressing in, setting goals, having purpose, resisting the enemy and standing against demonic agenda.

Greek philosophy in western Christianity has been destructive in some ways to America both in the political and in preventing the occurrence of miracles, signs and wonders. While the ungodly conquer different spheres of influence much of the church is passive, asleep, or content just keeping to its little corner, with no clear cut vision or purpose to impact society. It really is time for believers in Jesus to be united to take back politics, education, media, etc. It can only happen with vision, purpose and clear cut goals birthed from heaven.

I believe it is apparent in scripture that God desires to reveal our future to us. If we enter into an intimate relationship with Him, He will speak to us about our future in order to fill our lives with vision, purpose, passion and goals. If we do not desire that intimacy with Him, we might never know the future He has planned for us. We will just walk through this life blindly not knowing our destiny or purpose in life.

Once again Jesus speaking of Holy Spirit, *"But when He, the Spirit of Truth (the truth giving spirit) comes, He will guide you into all truth-the whole full truth, for He will not speak His own message-on His own authority-but will tell whatever He hears (from the Father, He will give the message that has been given to Him) and He will announce and **declare to you** the things that are to come- that will **happen in the future*** (John 16:13 Amp version)." Verses 14 and 15 go on to say that Holy Spirit will "reveal (declare, disclose and transmit) it to you."

Jeremiah 33:3 reads, *"Call to Me, and I will answer you and show you great and mighty things which you do not know."* The amplified version says He will show you things that are fenced and hidden.

Isaiah 42:9 says, *"Behold the former things have come to pass, and new things I declare; before they spring forth I tell you of them."* The word **declare** in Hebrew means to announce, predict and rehearse. God wants to reveal and disclose our future to us, things we do to know of before they occur, so that we know what He wants us to do, making us a motivated people fulfilling our destiny.

When we enter into a place of intimacy with Him, we will most certainly hear His voice. Romans 10:17 says, *"So then faith comes by hearing, and hearing by the word* (Rhema) *of God."* Here the word Rhema means the spoken word of God. Once we hear God's 'still small voice' as we seek Him, there will be enough faith and power available to bring that spoken word to pass.

How to Fulfill the Vision

Habakkuk 2:2-3 says, *"Then the Lord answered me and said: "Write the vision And make it plain on tablets, That he may run who reads it. For the **vision is yet for an appointed time;** But at the end it will speak, and it will not lie. Though it tarries, **wait** for it;* (Hebrew-**become one with it, portray, carve on the inside**) *Because it will surely come, It will not tarry."*

In the above scripture we are encouraged to write down the vision. Why? So we behold it, become one with it, causing it to go from our head to our hearts or spirit. The word vision in Hebrew means to **gaze at mentally, to perceive, to prophesy and to behold.**

Verse 3 says that the vision is for an appointed time. This is where many miss it, not understanding the timing of the vision. Usually when God gives us a vision, prophecy, goal, or purpose it is for a set time in our lives that has been pre-ordained before the foundation of this world. Be aware of that set time and do not jump the gun!

Many look for the immediate fulfillment of a prophecy from the Lord, without any preparation or becoming one with that vision or purpose. Thus they are not adequately prepared for the task and end up getting the job half done or fail completely.

We have to grasp the importance of tarrying or preparation when God shows us something. It is akin to incubation. Without the necessary incubation period the thing can be birthed prematurely and fail. Isaiah 42:9 talked of God **declaring new things to us.** As mentioned earlier the Hebrew word also refers to rehearsing it. What does rehearsing it imply? It entails going over something time and time again till we get it right. Then when the time comes to actually perform it we are able to so efficiently, without any setbacks.

Prophecy, visions and God given goals are easily accomplished and fulfilled when performed in His time, in His strength and when we prepare for and carve what He shows us in our hearts, minds and spirit.

Time and Chance

Ecclesiastes 9:10-12 says, *Whatever your hand finds to do, do it with your might... I returned and saw under the sun that— The race is not to the swift, Nor the battle to the strong, Nor bread to the wise, Nor riches to men of understanding, Nor favor to men of skill; But **time and chance happen to them all.** For man also does not know his time:...* ' It is essential that whatever we are called to do we give it 100%. We cannot give something 100% unless we are sure that is what we are called to do. Thus we need to know our purpose and what God has called us to do. It is only then that the God given purpose will motivate us to reach the goal and give it 100%.

Notice verse 11. Many think that the swift will win the race, or the strong the battle, or one with skill and ability will be put over and have the riches. God says this is not necessarily true. **Time and chance** happen to all of us. Verse 12 tells us that *man also does not know his time.* The bottom line is being at the right place as the right time. We call it **divine appointments.** Even if we do not have the quickness, strength, or skills we can still be put over. How? Understand that time and chance are in the Lord's hands. Pretty much everything I am doing today in ministry I had no natural ability to do. Yet somehow God has put me over in ministry, given me the ability to do things I never dreamed of doing, simply by having purpose and being in tune to time and chance.

God knows the future.   If we spend time seeking Him and getting to know Holy Spirit, we can be in tune to time and chance and know the future. Being at the right place at the time does not happen by being passive, lazy or having a whatever will be will be attitude. We have to do our part, God does His or has done His part and thereby we will be where He has preordained us to be before the foundation of the world.

*And we know that all things work together for good to those who love God, to those who are the **called according to His purpose*** (Romans 8:28). When we fit into our purpose in life all things can work together for our good. Many have taken this key verse intentionally out of context (partly because the negative influence of Greek philosophy injected into western Christianity). Many think that all things good or evil work together for the good no matter what. This is simply not true! Look at two key parts of this verse. First not all of us have all things working together for our good unless for the most part we are **actively pursuing and fitting into the purpose God has set for our lives.**

Fulfilling one's destiny and purpose does not simply fall out of the sky because God is sovereign. One has to make a conscious decision to pursue and fit into that purpose. Yes, God is sovereign! But who did He put in charge of this earth? Himself or mankind! Mankind was given control of this earth (see Genesis 1:26-28 & Psalm 115:16). That is why God the Creator, Jesus Himself had to born on this earth. In order to have authority on planet earth He had to put on flesh and blood. Why? Because He gave authority to those who were born on this planet. He also had to learn to operate in partnership with Holy Spirit to carry out His God given authority and then get our authority back from the Devil. *How God anointed Jesus of Nazareth with the Holy Spirit and with power, who went about doing good and healing all who were oppressed by the devil, for God was with Him* (Acts 10:38).

Also notice the first word in verse 28. *'And'!* That means something is tied to this verse. In context Romans 8:26-28 talks of allowing Holy Spirit to pray through us **in the Spirit,** (Greek refers to unknown tongues) this is one of His purposes for our life and helps us tap into our purpose. When Holy Spirit is allowed to pray through us, He makes intercession according to God's perfect will. *Now this is the confidence that we have in Him, that if we* **ask anything according to His will, He hears us.** *And if we know that He hears us, whatever we ask, we know that we have the petitions that we have asked of Him.* (1 John 5:14-15). If He is praying through us according to God's perfect will, then yes all things can work together for good.

In the Spring of 1978 my sole goal was to play football, but once I was baptized in Holy Spirit and spoke in tongues for the first time in my life my whole life turned around. From that first night of praying in tongues my steps were supernaturally ordered into world evangelism. People started getting saved and to this present day I have had the opportunity to lead over 200,000 people to Christ either one on one or in our outreaches overseas. When we pray in tongues Holy Spirit makes intercession for us according to God's perfect will for our lives. That is what happened to me. *And we know that all things work together for good to those who love God, to those who are the **called according to His purpose*** (Romans 8:28).

Forks in the Road

Many of us come to forks in the road in our journey through this life. A life void of vision and purpose will be filled with confusion, anxiety, procrastination, hopelessness and much more when those forks appear. Why? Because one does not know which way to go. The result can be either going down the wrong path leading to a lot of unhappiness and failure or fearfully refusing to go down any fork in the road, thereby stagnating. Both can be dead ends.

When one is filled with vision and purpose the forks in the

road are not accompanied with confusion, as we have sought the Lord, heard His voice and are ready for any changes in our lives because we know which direction to go. It's our destiny!

In the Fall of 1985 I was on a ministry trip to minister in a number of churches in Montana and Minnesota. I decided to spend a few days fasting and praying while ministering in a small church in Billings, Montana. I recalled a message I had heard in a small church called City on the Hill in a southern suburb of Denver, Colorado. The Pastor preached a very short message on the '**Motivating Force of Purpose.**' It turned out to be a Rhema word for me from Heaven that took my life and our ministry to a whole new level and launched me into my destiny.

While in Billings I drove up to the foothills north of the city and spent a lot of time praying and asking God for purpose and vision for my life. I was listening to a song by **David Meece** called '**YOU CAN GO.**' The words of that song were like God's audible voice to my spirit man. Holy Spirit said through this powerful song *"Mark it time for you to go now. You have the power of God let it flow. You have the treasure world wants to know. It's time to take it to the nations."* It was so powerful to hear that still small voice so clearly through that song. I got in my car and like it says in Habakkuk 2:2-3 I wrote the vision down on a piece of paper and taped it to the dashboard of my car. Every time I got into the car I saw the vision before me and said *"You to go now. You have the power of God let it flow. You have the treasure world wants to know. Time to take it to the nations."* I began to run with this vision.

From Billings I drove to Minneapolis, Minnesota to preach at Church on the Move. It was pastored by Mark E. Anderson. He had spent much time with evangelistic ministries, as a campaign coordinator. Now he was organizing outreaches into India. He asked if I wanted to go to India in February 1986 and conduct an open air outreaches. Within a couple of days I said count me in. Keep in mind our ministry was really struggling financially in those days. I had never been overseas and never raised funds for something so large. I had many doors opening up to preach in the USA, Canada and to do other things. When he invited me to go to India I had many forks in the road. Which way do I go? I knew exactly what I was to do! Why? Because I had sought Holy Spirit and He spoke clearly to me what He wanted me to do while I was in the foothills, just outside of Billings.

Long story short the money came in supernaturally and I was on my first mission trip overseas in my life. I saw powerful miracles and 5,500 people came to Christ in my outreach.

For the first time in my life I saw God open blind eyes. I was hooked. I have been addicted to world missions ever since. It was in seeking God for purpose, vision and goals that turned my circumstances around and set me on my course for life. By having purpose and vision I was able to navigate clearly through the forks in the road. Purpose can set you on the path to success.

By the way many people for many years, even recently have gotten Mark E. Anderson and I mixed up. He is Mark E. Anderson and works with Youth with a Mission and 'Call to All' doing tremendous work. I am Mark R. Anderson. I thank God for Mark and how God used him to launch me into my purpose and destiny.

Jesus was a man of purpose. ...*For **this purpose** the Son of God was manifested, that He might destroy the works of the devil.* (1 John 3:8). Aren't you glad that Jesus was a man of purpose and He stuck to His purpose in life regardless of circumstances? He was not sidetracked from fulfilling that purpose or by becoming an earthly king at that time, even though He would be coming back to rule and reign on this earth, as King one day. He did not die a premature death. Everything He did was in keeping with His purpose and vision in life.

Now the question is: Will you stick to your purpose in this life and fulfill the vision God has for you? Ecclesiastes 3:1 says

*To everything there is a season, A **time for every purpose** under heaven.* There is a season for the fulfillment of that purpose and vision that God has for your life. Jesus did not get sidetracked from His purpose. Will you fit in to your purpose or will it pass you by because you were not in tune to that season and purpose? It is up to you! Holy Spirit longs to be your partner and tell you or transmit to your spirit things that pertain to the future as you pray in the spirit and draw close to Him.

Understanding purpose and vision has in many ways transformed this ministry at different times as well as our personal lives. It will work for you as well, when you understand the seasons and purpose for which you were created by God. Don't get sidetracked by a religious spirit. It will take you off course with the destiny and purpose God has placed on your life. Stick to your purpose and destiny by living your life for His Audience only!

CHAPTER 10

Getting Beyond Our Religious Boxes

*If we **let Him alone** like this, everyone will believe in Him* (John 11:48).

What a profound statement made by the religious leaders, who hated Jesus. Sharmila and I do our best to get out of the way and let Jesus, or Holy Spirit alone to do what they do best miracles, healings, signs, wonders, salvations, etc. This is key to success in ministry. This statement was made in reference to Jesus raising Lazarus from the dead. A miracle working Jesus is an unstoppable Jesus. There is one problem here. Religion and some Christians try to put Jesus in a box. Religion wants to shut Him down. I have news for you. He is not in anyone's religious box, nor will He ever climb inside a box with anyone. We can never ever put

Him in a box. He is limitless! We sometimes try to limit Him by staying inside our religious boxes. He is outside the box. Get out of your box and rise up to where He is.

The heaven, even the heavens, are the Lord's; But the earth He has given to the children of men (Psalm 115:16). He gave authority to mankind to rule and reign on this earth. In order for Holy Spirit be limitless in our world. We need to get out of our boxes, quit trying to please man only and use our authority in partnership with Him. He gave us authority to work with Him (see Genesis 1:26-28 & Matthew 16:19).

As mentioned, The Father, Jesus and Holy Spirit are not in a box. It is pride and arrogance to think we can contain them in our little religious boxes, with our expression of who we think God is. Look at what Jesus said. This gives us a clue to why He was so successful in ministry. *Then Jesus answered and said to them, "**Most assuredly,** I say to you, the Son can **do nothing of Himself, but what He sees the Father do;** for whatever He does, **the Son also does** in like manner. For the Father loves the Son, and **shows Him all things that He Himself does;** and He will show Him **greater works than these,** that you may marvel. For as the **Father raises the dead** and gives life to them, even so the Son gives life to whom He will* (John 5:19-21). Jesus did not try to limit the Father to what the religious leaders thought the Father was like but listened carefully and followed the Father's every lead. It totally rubbed the religious leaders the wrong way because of the religious boxes they had placed God the Father in. We have the same problem in the church today. But Jesus sent Holy Spirit so we can follow Jesus' every lead and come out of our religious boxes (see John 14:12, 16:13-14).

Jesus also said to the religious leaders who were stuck in their boxes: *You search the Scriptures, for in them you think you have eternal life; and these are they which testify of Me.* ***But you are not willing to come to Me*** *that you may have life* (John 5:39-40). How sad. They just wanted to stay in their box, unwilling to come up to where He was. The religious spirit had a tremendous foothold in these leaders lives. They were very grounded in the word of God but at the same time so bound in pride and arrogance to think somehow they had cornered God in their religious box. Because of their pride they were totally clueless that the Messiah was in their midst. As mentioned earlier there are 70 major prophecies in the Old Testament about Jesus the Messiah coming to earth. They were unwilling to get out of their boxes of how they perceived God to be and they missed out. **Will you miss out on what Jesus wants to do?**

Jesus warned his closest followers to be aware of the religious spirit (the 'leaven of the scribes and pharisees'- see

Matthew 16:5-12) as we mentioned earlier. Do you think that might apply to those who follow Him today? How do you know if you are in a box and by your lifestyle you are literally trying to limit our limitless God? Mark 7:1-23 is where Jesus literally shows us how people give place to a religious spirit and left unchecked, it becomes a demonic stronghold. We shared about this in the opening chapters. The first seed to giving place to a religious spirit is finding fault, being judgemental or critical towards others (Chapter 2) who do not believe the way you do (see Mark 7:1-2).

The second seed is pride, arrogance and false humility (Chapter 3). When we, like the religious leaders think that God somehow has climbed into our box and somehow we have the cutting edge on what God is doing and everything revolves around us, watch out, it is a sure step towards a fall from grace (see Mark 7:3, James 4:6 & Proverbs 16:18).

The third step becomes a turning point towards the worse if we allow ourselves to go there. It is when we hold onto manmade traditions contrary to what Holy Spirit wants to do (Chapter 4). Many fall prey to this today in Christian circles. Many denominations were birthed out of a mighty move of Holy Spirit. But when people start to think God will only move in certain way because after all that is how He moved 100 years ago we are stuck in a religious box and God has to raise up others. That is why the Spirit of God is constantly looking for pliable vessels to work through. *For the eyes of the Lord run to and fro throughout the whole earth, to show Himself strong on behalf of those whose heart is loyal to Him* (2 Chronicles 16:9).

The last seed Jesus mentions (Chapter 5) is when it has become a religious or demonic stronghold. *For **laying aside the commandment of God,** you hold the tradition of men...* (Mark 7:8). There comes a point when so called Christians become so bound in their religious box with judging, pride, unteachablness, and keeping of tradition that they would sooner lay aside the word of God to keep their religious tradition. We see that all over the world with Christianity. A recent survey amongst various Christians confirmed this, most Christians would rather hold on to religious tradition than the word of God. Paul warned us in the last days the church would be *having **a form of godliness but denying its power.*** And from such people turn away or literally flee from them (see 2 Timothy 3:5)! God is not in it!

*Yes, again and again they **tempted God,** And **limited the Holy One** of Israel. **They did not remember His power:** The day when He redeemed them from the enemy* (Psalms 78:41-42). How did Israel tempt God? They did not remember His power. We can **tempt and limit God working** through us, by not working in partnership with Him to carry out His will on this earth **by being stuck in our little religious boxes.**

In Matthew 17:1- 9 Jesus was transfigured bright white with the glory of God. Moses and Elijah appeared by His side. Peter wanted to build three tabernacles and camp there. Jesus was not interested in camping out or monuments. He is interested in movement. There are many places in this world with monuments to what God did in the past, but totally dead with no movement today. It is time we let go of our pride and get out our religious boxes, follow Jesus in what He is doing and see a lasting move of God. Quit doing things for show! It will not happen without laying down our selfish pride, arrogance and getting out our manmade boxes.

We wonder why He is not moving. It is because He wants us to quit camping where the last move of God took place and move with what He is doing today. Many times we limit the move of God by living in the past, doing good religious things. We keep real busy but all we are doing is wasting time looking good. Rather than doing a good thing, how about doing a God thing? The meaning of insanity, doing something over and over again with no results. That is what cold dead religion is like. Quit flogging a dead horse. Dismount!

Many mighty moves of God have taken place. The problem that arises many times to prematurely shut down the move of God is that people come along and out of pride and the flesh start to seek after the signs, wonders, gifts, blessings or feelings to put on a show, rather than seeking after the gift giver or blesser Himself. Many people seek after healing. What is better to seek after healing or the Healer Himself and get Him? Seek Him! You get the Healer. Along with that comes healing, signs, wonders, miracles, joy, peace, populating heaven and much more. It is time to turn up our passion and pursuit of Jesus. He knows no limit or bounds. When you seek Him you have everything and you venture into where the impossible becomes possible. Don't get sidetracked by pride and end up in a box.

I like what my friend Mike Francen said in his book I Dare to Believe *"Don't put a question mark where God has put a period."* When we begin to question God we are climbing into a preconceived religious box. That is where we go wrong. It is time to rise up to where He is. Come out of your box. Mike also said *"You will never define the fulness of God's favor upon your life until you venture into the impossible."* To do that you need live life outside the box, work with Him, but at the same time let Him alone so all men will believe in Him. What is He telling you to do! Most world shakers have lived life outside the box, being who God made them to be. You were born an original. Don't leave this world a copy.

In closing let me share some things that will really blow the lids off those religious manmade boxes we try to put God in. Many times we limit God to what we have experienced in life. If we do not learn to walk by faith, realizing absolutely nothing is impossible for God, take the limits off Holy Spirit we will continue to not experience or see His glory manifested on this earth in miracles, signs and wonders. I hope this encourages you to take the limits off Holy Spirit.

Speaking of taking off the limits on Holy Spirit this is from my good friend and one of my favorite authors, Pastor Steve C. Shank's book **God Made Visible.** He shares some stories of the glory manifesting in Jim Roger's ministry (www.ExperiencingHisPresence.org). Here are some of Jim's experiences of the glory manifesting in different countries of the world. I had lunch with Jim Rogers while in Colorado as I was putting the finishing touches on this book. I asked him to pray over me to begin to experience the same things he shares below. I have experienced some of these things he mentions below but only on a small scale. I am taking the limit off Holy Spirit and expecting to see these kind of miracles in the days to come increase in a mighty way. All for His glory and honor!

LEPERS HEALED: "Some of the most dramatic times when

the glory manifests are when it can be seen as a visible, tangible cloud. One night we were holding a crusade in a stadium. As we praised the Lord, we saw what looked like a physical cloud coming into the stadium. It was about 35 feet across and 20 feet in diameter. We knew that this was the glory of God. This night a group of about 45 lepers were together, and none of the crowd wanted to get near them. The glory cloud descended and came down right on the lepers. It literally enveloped them—we couldn't see them for about fifteen minutes! We continued to praise Jesus, but everyone in the stadium was looking at the cloud. When it lifted off of them and ascended, every one of those former untouchables was completely healed—nothing missing and everything restored! What happened next blessed me the most. When the crowd saw what the Lord had done for these 45 people, they rushed around them and started hugging, embracing and expressing their love to them!"

DEAD RAISED: "I was at a house meeting for pastors, and we were discussing keys on how to continue in a move of God that was happening in this country. Suddenly there was knock on the door. Keep in mind, we were in a dangerous country and had kept our meeting place a secret. We opened the door, and here was a man holding his 8- year-old daughter's body in his arms. He was holding a piece of paper with our address on it, and he said the Holy Spirit spoke it to him and told him to bring her here for prayer. His daughter had died four days earlier in the village where they lived, and he had carried her body for four days to get to this address! The smell coming from her body was horrible, and she had taken on a dark grey color.

"We laid her on a large coffee table in the main room of the house, and I told the pastors to all pray at once over this girl. As we prayed, the presence of God became so thick that several of the pastors could not stand and dropped to their knees. You could see the room fill up with what looked like haze. All of a sudden the little girl's eyes fluttered, and she sat up! In the time it took her to sit up, God restored her skin, and she was completely fine.

"We all praised God for about 20 minutes, and then there was another knock on the door. When we opened the door, another man and his friend were carrying his dead teenage son on a stretcher. He was holding a piece of paper as well—the Lord had also given him our address! His son was lying there in his underwear and had been shot in the chest three days earlier. This time the national pastors were very confident and told this father to lay his son on the coffee table. We gathered around him, started to pray, and the presence became very thick again with haze filling the room. All of a sudden the teenager's body began to bounce up and down on the table! I seriously thought that the table was going to shatter. As we watched his body bounce, all of a sudden his eyes opened. God had brought life back into his body. The father had brought with him a pair of *pants and a shirt for his son to wear home—faith!"*

Jim Rogers emailed me a few more testimonies to share of what Holy Spirit is doing in these days. I remember hearing prophecies when I was just entering into ministry that in last days these kind of miracles would start taking place.

Jim sharing *"The first time that I saw the limbs go out, was at a pastors conference. It was during worship. A pastor was praising God with his hands up in the air. His right hand was missing and had a piece of leather over the stub. Lord spoke to me, and told me he wanted to grow his hand back out. I could not get over to lay hands on him. It was too crowded, so I went up on the stage and commanded his hand to grow out. Suddenly the leather Popped off and this ball formed up out of his wrist. Then suddenly he turned his hand around and there were fingers on it and he was wiggling them in the air. The people around him went crazy.*

Later that night we were at the crusade. There was about 120 or 150 people missing one of their legs or they were on crutches. The pastors and I looked at each other and said if God can grow the hand out then he can grow a leg out. We started to command legs to grow. Suddenly one of the legs shot down and began to form a foot. We couldn't believe what we had just seen. We were like Lord show it to us again. Suddenly the leg started to grow out and one by one they started coming down and forming legs. Shortly all of the people had your legs back. They came down front and put the crutches a pile it was over 15 feet tall.

Another time we were ministering in the Brothels, we came in and saw a body laying underneath the sheet, we knew it was one of the girls. Next to her was a paramedic sitting on a stool. We went over and asked him what happened. He told us that he thought she had just died from a heart attack about an hour and a half or maybe two hours before. We asked him why haven't you removed the body. He told us he was waiting for the Coroner to come. We asked if we could pray for her. He was a Buddhist and didn't understand what we are asking. He said OK. We gathered around her to pray the three men that were with me stood behind her and I set down next to her on the floor as we started to pray you could feel the presence of God fall in the room. It was almost like it was a cloud around us. Suddenly she sat up, God had brought her back to life. Her friends were getting very excited in the back and one of our men went and talked to them and they got saved. The Paramedic fainted and fell on the floor. He was OK but didn't understand what just happened.

I asked the Mama Sans in charge if there was a place we can go and talk to the young girl. They took us to a very nice room so we could talk to her. As were walking into the room I had my arm around her and told her everything was going to be OK. She looked up at me and said I know your voice. The three men with me were quite loud as we walked in. She turned around and said I know all of your voices. Then she told us in her own words what happened. She said she had a heart attack and died. Then she fell backwards into a pit. When she landed in the pit she was surrounded by demons. Their job was to torture and abuse her. It was the smell of burning and rotting flesh. It made her throw up several times. I said I don't know if you've heard the Gospel before. She knew she had made a mistake because she was a Buddhist. She said she just knew it was wrong. She said the demons were abusing her when all of a sudden she heard the four of us start praying and as we started to pray, the demons left her. The demons were trying to figure out how to stop what happened. As we continued to pray suddenly a giant hand came down with a white robe on it, and grabbed her arm and that's when she sat up. The Lord had brought her back to life."

CHAPTER 11

Being A Well Balanced Believer

Understanding the importance of being a well balanced, non-compromising believers has helped us to be successful in ministry and our personal life. To be physically healthy we need to have a well balanced diet. An imbalanced diet can lead to health problems. It is the same with our Christian walk! *For God did not give us a spirit of timidity of cowardice of craven and cringing and fawning and fear – but He has given us a spirit of power and of love and of calm and **well balanced mind** and discipline and self control* (2 Timothy 1:7Amp). This verse clearly defines that God has given us a sound, well balanced mind to combat fear and to live a victorious life as a follower of Jesus Christ.

The Bible displays the multifaceted nature of God. Unfortunately our problem is that being human we tend to get narrow minded and many times unable to fathom, grasp, or comprehend the many facets of the Almighty. We are stuck in our preconceived religious boxes. When He reveals Himself to believers in a certain way we tend to think that revelation only is the cure all to every problem for many years to come. With that mentality we tend to jump from one ditch to another ditch, stuck in a rut. We are no longer **"well balanced or sound minded."**

An over emphasis of only one facet of our multi-faceted God can take us off the road, put us in a ditch stuck in a rut. A religious spirit will cause many believers to replace pursuing Jesus for just a single facet or expression of God. They turn that single expression into an idol. You can have a part of Jesus or all of Jesus. Why get stuck on a single facet of Jesus when you can have all of Him, just by simply pursuing Him and following His leading?

Every Wind of Doctrine

It is time for the Body of Christ to grow up! We need to get on track and on the road so we can get somewhere as believers. Riding in the ditch does not permit us to go very far or fast. Ephesians 4:11- 14 says, *He Himself gave some to be **apostles, some prophets, some evangelists, and some pastors and teachers,** for the **equipping** of the saints for the **work of ministry,** for the **edifying*** *of the body of Christ, till we come to the **unity of the faith** and of the knowledge of the Son of God, to **a perfect** (Greek- **mature**) man, to the measure of the **stature of the fullness of Christ;** that we should no longer be **children, tossed to and fro and carried about with every wind of doctrine...***

Ephesians 4:8 says that God has given *"gifts to men."* Verse 11 tells us what these gifts are? Not all of us have the same gifts. Verse 12 informs us that these ministry gifts are for the purpose of equipping, building and edifying the body of Christ to perform the work of the ministry. Verse 13 and 14 tell us that these gifts are given to help us to grow up and prevent us from being tossed from one ditch to the other. Don't get stuck just gleaning from one expression of God. There are many giftings in the Body of Christ we can glean from.

Imbalance is a problem we have in the Body of Christ, when following man more than Jesus. Then becoming isolated or into only one stream of expression. It will cause many to walk in deception, arrogance and pride with a know it all attitude. I love gleaning from many different streams in the Body of Christ to get balance. I never want to follow a man more than Jesus. Too many believers have and if the person they follow falls they fall with them. I have watched many Christian's lives fall apart this way when the emphasis was the one man show or one stream.

We need each other for proper balance.

Many pastors and churches do not make use of the five-fold ministry gifts. Then on the other side many believers gravitate towards specific ministry gifts and do not have a healthy spiritual balance. A religious spirit will seek to keep us imbalanced spiritually. One thing I have noticed in the five-fold ministry gifts, especially of teachers, prophets, and evangelists (including myself) is that God puts a burning desire to minister and emphasize a certain doctrine for a period of time. For example, God has called me to primarily minister on healing, faith, missions, humility, etc. If people gravitated only towards my teachings they would be very imbalanced. I am merely being obedient in sharing the revelation that Holy Spirit has given me. I admit that I am limited, but flow in the gifting Holy Spirit has put in my life. It is important to learn from other ministry gifts. Even though I am called to teach and minister in certain areas I desire all of God. **We need each other for proper balance.** I have to glean from others just to stay balanced myself.

Another reason many Christians are in the ditch is because they learn from one ministry "gifting" or teaching and maybe have found freedom from bondages in their lives through that expression. They begin to believe that teaching is the cure to all problems for the entire body of Christ. Some become so extreme and zealous in their doctrine that others in the Body of Christ want to have nothing to do with what they believe even though there is truth in their belief. Unfortunately this is a classic example of one camp riding the ditch with their extreme beliefs and the other camp also riding the ditch by avoiding that doctrine, not embracing it at all. Both are imbalanced and giving place to a religious spirit. Those who are repelled by the extreme need to "cease throwing the baby out with the bathwater." Those who are given to extremes need to understand that there is more to Christianity than just a single facet of God that has helped them out.

Extreme - vs - Balance

Many have learned about the power of faith and have experienced its productive results in their lives. If that is all they embrace, to the exclusion of other beliefs, then they take it to an extreme. I have 'been there and done that' in the early years of ministry. Occasionally those who have witnessed the extremes and abuse in the faith movement have chosen not to embrace faith and/or healing, and instead have become very critical of those who do. Hebrews 11:6 says, *"**without** (Greek – **outside of**) **faith it is impossible to please God,** for he who comes to God must believe that He is, and that **He is a rewarder** of those who **diligently seek Him.**"* It is very clear even if someone is imbalanced with the faith message we should not disregard it ourselves; rather we *'walk by faith'* (see 2 Corinthians 5:7). Unless we do so we cannot please God. Everyone should embrace faith for the simple reason that it pleases God and it is one of the basic foundations of Christianity (see Hebrews 6:1).

Pursue Jesus More...

In some churches or groups God has moved sovereignly with many miracles, signs and wonders because they were hungry for God and had pure hearts before Him but maybe no solid word base. I have seen the move of the Spirit die down in these circles because rather than being driven by a hunger for the presence of Christ and His Word, they start to seek after the manifestations or feelings first. We need to seek first Christ and His kingdom. Not the manifestations, blessings, feelings, gifts, power, etc first. In Christ is all of these things but if we seek first these things more than Christ then they become a religious idol. This is also putting the cart before the horse. Jesus said in Matthew 6:33 ***"Seek first the kingdom** of God and His righteousness, and **all these other things will be added** unto you."* Notice Jesus tells us do not seek first the things or the blessings. Seek first God and His kingdom and secondly you can believe for the 'things' and they will be added. We need to have the right perspective in going after and seeking *'these things.'* **Seek and pursue Him first and you will**

have everything He is.

It is best to glean from, learn from and gravitate towards leaders who are actively, passionately pursuing Jesus, who are not looking for the glory of man but the glory of God. When you truly seek Jesus healing, signs, and wonders come with Him. This is what Sharmila and I have done and is the reason we are licensed and ordained by Randy Clark and Bill Johnson, because we want to be under that covering of humble men who are pursuing Jesus more than than the manifestations and blessings. As a result of their pursuit of Jesus millions around this globe have been swept into the Kingdom, not to mention all the signs, wonders, miracles and including the dead being raised, just as we have seen in India since the time when we hosted Randy Clark there.

When men and women pursue power, giftings, manifestations more than Christ and then people begin gravitating towards or pursuing them for the gifting, they have created an atmosphere for arrogance and the religious spirit to thrive and grow. You also set up people for the fall from grace because gifting should never be pursued more than character and Christ Himself.

The Right Balance on Prosperity

Once Steve Valentine, pastor of a large church from Missoula,

Montana stated at a conference I attended that for many years he and his church did not believe in the faith or prosperity message and taught against those beliefs (maybe because of seeing the extremes). With humility he said he began to realize the foolishness of his beliefs as he pondered the opposite of faith and prosperity are unbelief and poverty. He said he did not want to declare the beliefs of his church to be a church of unbelief and poverty. Hebrews 11:6 says *Without faith it is impossible to please God.* He began to embrace a healthy balance of faith and prosperity. God began to bless and manifest His presence in their midst in a powerful way when this balance came about in his church.

I definitely believe in the right prosperity message because it is God's word. Psalm 35:27 says, "... *Let the Lord be magnified, who has* **pleasure in the prosperity of His servants.**" 3 John:2 says, "*Beloved, I pray that you may* **prosper in all things** *and be in health, just as your soul prospers.*" This scripture makes it very apparent that God desires His servants to prosper. At the same time He does not want us to be consumed by money. I have witnessed ministries in the USA and overseas consumed with prosperity or the prosperity message that were laced with greed and selfishness, rather than a desire to use it for the Kingdom of Christ. James 4:3 says, "*You ask and do not receive, because you ask amiss that you may spend it on* **your pleasure.**"

Money is like electricity. It can be used for good or if used incorrectly can bring harm (see 2 Timothy 3:2, 1 Timothy 6:10). Many have looked at extreme prosperity beliefs and concluded that the prosperity message is from the devil. They go way to the other extreme teaching people that to be poor is the will of God. Many are influenced by this religious tradition that was taught by Augustine in 400AD when Christianity became greatly influenced by Greek philosophy. Religious traditions of men teach if you want to be humble, then you have to be poor. Yet the word says *By **humility** and the fear of the Lord Are **riches** and honor and life* (Proverbs 22:4). With this poverty mindset they do not get much done for the kingdom of God as they do not have the financial ability to do so. This is once again a good example of 'ditch riding' Christianity.

We need to be balanced in godly prosperity. We need to get out of the ditch and get on the road? Then we would see God's perspective on prosperity. Humility with the fear and the reverence of God is like a magnet that attracts wealth (see 1 Timothy 6:17-19). The balance: is not for the purpose of being a selfish wealth consumer but for the sake of being a wealth generator to spread the Gospel. God gives wealth to get the Gospel out to the nations and be a blessings to those in need.

Pendulum Swingers

I have heard ministers teach a particular doctrine to an extreme and then within a couple of years teach against that very doctrine, now promoting a different one. All they have done is jumped from one ditch to another. It is time to get in the middle of the road and on track with what God wants to do. Many Christians have become like a pendulum swinging going from one extreme to the other.

2 Corinthians 2:11 says *lest Satan should take advantage of us; for we are **not ignorant of his devices.*** From this verse and many others it shows we need to be aware of the demonic realm. I have watched people on both sides of the road on this doctrine. Some just ignore demons and what Satan does and do not live in reality of the real world. Others get too focused on demons and Satan like a young minister I heard preaching to a congregation one time saying *"the devil is always one step ahead of us."* He was saying this to believers who were beaten up by demons to justify their predicament. 1 John 4:4 says *You are of God, little children, and* **have overcome them,** *because* **He who is in you is greater** *than he who is in the world.*

Compromise is False Balance

Some may incorrectly believe that a balanced Christian is one who has to compromise his beliefs. Not at all! Keep the passion burning! Being balanced does not entail compromising one's beliefs because others take us to be too extreme. It means that we should balance our teachings and beliefs with all the various aspects of God's word, not to water down the word of God.

*Finally my brethren, be **strong in the Lord** and the power of His might. Put on the **whole armor of God** that you may be able to stand against the **wiles of the devil.** For we do not wrestle against flesh and blood, but against principalities, against powers, against the rulers of the darkness of this age, against spiritual hosts of wickedness in the heavenly places. Therefore take up the **whole armor of God,** that you may be **able to withstand** in the evil day, and having done all to stand. Stand therefore, having girded your waist with truth, having put on the breastplate of righteousness, and having shod your feet with the preparation of the gospel of peace; above all, taking the shield of faith with which you will be able to quench all the fiery darts of the wicked one. And take the helmet of salvation, and the sword of the Spirit, which is the word of God; praying always with all prayer and supplication in the Spirit, being watchful to this end with all perseverance and supplication for all the saints* (Ephesians 6:10-18).

Verse 10 encourages us to be *strong in the Lord.* We can be strong in the Lord by being well balanced. The armor of God speaks to me about balance and having everything God wants me to have to be spiritually healthy and follow Christ.

Verse 11 and 13 tells us to put on the whole armor of God. Today many Christians are only partially clad spiritually; in other words they are half naked spiritually. For instance, they may have faith, but forget the rest of the armor. Some may have the helmet of salvation but not the shield of faith. They enter into battle, wondering why they are ineffective and powerless.

So much of God's word is interconnected. An example, in order to have effective faith we need to have love (see Galatians 5:6). Faith without love is useless (see 1 Corinthians 13). 2 Peter 1:5-7 tells us *But also for this very reason, giving all diligence, add to your faith virtue, to virtue knowledge, to knowledge self-control, to self-control perseverance, to perseverance godliness, to godliness brotherly kindness, and to brotherly kindness love. 2 Peter 1:8-9 says, "for if these things are yours and abound, you will be **neither barren nor unfruitful** in the knowledge of our Lord Jesus Christ. For **he who lacks these things is short sighted** even to blindness, and forgotten that he was cleansed from his old sins."*

Ephesians 6:12 gives us insight into our battle with demonic forces. Verse 11 encourages us to stand against the wiles (Greek – lies and strategies) of the devil and demons. The best way to keep from demonic deception is to be a well balanced Christian who embraces all aspects of God's Word. We combat the devil and his demonic lies with the truth of God's Word.

Paul warns Timothy about the last days. *For the time will come when they will not endure sound doctrine, but according to their own desires, because they **have itching ears,** they will heap up for themselves teachers; and they will turn their ears away from the truth, and be turned aside to fables* (2 Timothy 4:3-4). Don't just run after things that itch your ears and take you off course. Be balanced, uncompromising by being filled with Holy Spirit, guided by His word, truth and pursue Jesus passionately.

If you have been in the Lord for awhile you have probably heard how some people are so Spirit oriented they are flakey, wacky and fruity. They tend to blow in and blow out. Or on the other hand you have people so word oriented only they dry up, are stale and Holy Spirit is not moving in their life. Wouldn't it be neat to see a new breed of believers raised up who have a healthy balance without compromise of God's word working in their life, full of Holy Spirit and passionately pursuing Father, Son, Holy Spirit, going in the direction Holy Spirit wants them to go. We should not live on yesterday's victories but live for what Holy Spirit is doing today, following His leading, just like Jesus followed Father God's lead (see John 5:19-21).

Religion: Enemy of God or Relationship?

CHAPTER 12

The Great Rewards For Integrity

There are leaders called to greatness in God's Kingdom and they will greatly impact nations because they have placed a strong emphasis on character as well as hungered for Christ's presence, nature and power in their life. At the same time there are leaders called to greatness in God's Kingdom around the world who if they refuse to deal with character issues they could very well end up falling short of reaching their full potential in Christ. In certain nations God is starting to unleash His power and Spirit in a measure we have not witnessed before. Will you be ready to used by Him?

Many times when dealing with a religious spirit that lives for the praises of men more than the praises of God dishonesty, exaggeration, hype, and outright lying become part of the mix. After all they are not living for the Audience of the ONE and ONLY! They live to promote themselves and elevate themselves so the means justifies the end. They portray to the world something they are not but they obtain the praises and honor of man, which they desire. The further we go down that path the more diabolical and dark we become and the religious spirit gains a foothold in our life.

There are things leaders need to be aware of both good and bad to be the most effective for Christ. Often in Full Gospel circles there is a strong emphasis on the gifts or the giftings God has placed on one's life. That is good but if we place a greater emphasis on the giftings then our character we can eventually fall short of the mark.

I have been in ministry since 1978 and involved in mission work throughout the world since 1981 on a regular basis. I have watched many ministries all over the world allow their giftings to surpass their character and end up falling into great sin or fall by the wayside (no longer in ministry or having a great ministry) despite having tremendous giftings and the call of God on their life. Because these leaders did not put an emphasis on humility and integrity one after another have fallen in this past 125 years. It has become like a domino effect but sad to say many will not learn from these mistakes and will repeat them. Many driven by arrogance and a religious spirit continue to downplay the need on placing character above gifting. For many all it has become is a religious show. They are driven by performance to look good. Where will that take you? Down a dead end road!

Jesus said in the last days before He would return that *many will be **offended,** will betray one another, and will hate one another* (Matthew 24:10). The Greek word for offended also means scandalized. In other words there will be many scandals. Christian leaders are not exempt from this. Many Christian leaders have fallen from grace. Mainly because they did not deal with the little foxes (character issues) in their life that spoiled the vine. These scandals do not mean the Holy Spirit will not do some very powerful things in the days to come. It is time to get ready for a powerful move of Holy Spirit! There are pockets in the world right now where it is crucial that the spiritual atmosphere be set because Holy Spirit is ready to move in ways never witnessed before in those areas. India is one of those regions.

I want to share with you some key things that will take leaders very far and also at the same time show you why so many leaders are falling today. Here in America passionate followers of Christ are taught to be people of integrity and honesty. Our country was founded by godly leaders like Presidents George

Washington and Abraham Lincoln who could not bring themselves to lie. They put a strong emphasis on integrity and honesty. Mahatma Ghandi was a man of similar principles. I believe that is what made him such a great leader. These were the kind of men who would tell the truth even to their own hurt. They were not self serving looking for power and control but cared for the people. They have passed on a great heritage and legacy for others to follow.

As a follower of Jesus Christ I am greatly attracted to leaders with great integrity. America has been changing though in recent years as well as other countries. Integrity and humility are no longer virtues to pursue. Lying and covering up lies especially in the politics and the media has taken our nation downhill rapidly. Lying and dishonesty is at an all-time high. Much of this has crept into all areas of society and including the church. Do we hunger for truth and integrity in a world full of lies? This is what can set us apart from the rest if we do.

2 Thessalonians 2:9-12 says that in the last days many (all over the world) will lack integrity and believe lies. *The coming of the lawless one is according to the working of Satan, with all power, signs, and **lying wonders,** and with all **unrighteous deception** among those who perish, because **they did not receive the love of the truth, that they might be saved.** And for this reason **God***

will send them strong delusion, that they should believe the lie, that they all may be condemned who did not believe the truth but had pleasure in unrighteousness. Lying and deception is part of ushering in the spirit of Anti-Christ as they follow the father of lies, the Devil himself. A good example of this kind of spirit today is Hillary Clinton. The media and many of her followers despite her being caught in lie after lie don't care. They do their best, to cover up for her. When this kind of deception comes from the top what will it do to the nation? Proverbs 29:12 says *If a ruler pays attention to lies,* **All his servants become wicked.**

Satan is the Father of lies, as Jesus said in John 8:44. *You are of your father the devil, and the desires of your father you want to do. He was a murderer from the beginning, and **does not stand in the truth,** because there is **no truth in him. When he speaks a lie, he speaks from his own resources, for he is a liar and the father of it.***

Let us do just the opposite of Satan and his followers. *Lest Satan should take advantage of us; for we are not ignorant of his devices* (2 Corinthians 2:11). Let's passionately pursue truth. Let us not be part of the many who lack integrity and believe and spread lies. As a whole passionate believers of Jesus Christ should hate lying and deceit. Let's take a look at what the scriptures say about these matters and see the great blessing there is in being a person of integrity.

The Importance of Truth

First let's look at the importance of truth. *Jesus said I am the way, THE TRUTH, and the life. No one comes to the Father except through me* (John 14:6). One thing Jesus is, is **TRUTH.** We can not say we are truly his disciples unless we are people of **TRUTH.**

In John 16:13 Jesus said this about the Holy Spirit, *However, when He, the **Spirit of truth,** has come, He will **guide you into all truth;** for He will not speak on His own authority, but whatever He hears He will speak; and He will **tell you things to come.*** Holy Spirit is the Spirit of **TRUTH.** He will guide us into all truth. He will show us things to come. The Greek says He will **transmit to your spirit things that pertain the future.**

In the scriptures Holy Spirit is also referred to as a dove. Doves are gentle but very skittish birds. Pastor Bill Johnson was sharing on this and said *"We always need to walk keeping the Dove* (Holy Spirit) *in mind."* There are things that grieve Holy Spirit. We need to be people always mindful of His presence if we are to walk in greater power and glory. *In all your ways **acknowledge Him,** And He shall **direct your paths*** (Proverbs 3:6). When He directs your steps many times heaven invading earth follows.

Numbers 23:19 -20 says *"God is not a man, that He should lie, Nor a son of man, that He should repent. Has He said, and will He not do? Or has He **spoken,** and will He not **make it good?** Behold, I have received a command to bless; He has blessed, and I cannot reverse it.* It is impossible for God to lie. For God to lie the universe would fall apart. He is *upholding all things by the word of His power* (Hebrews 1:3). We are made in His likeness and image to be like Him. Our words have to be words of integrity, honesty and authority. *Therefore be imitators of God as dear children* (Ephesians 5:1).

God speaking in Psalm 89:34 says *My **covenant I will not break,** Nor **alter the word** that has gone out of My lips.* The highest form of any covenant ever made is a blood covenant. What God the Father has done through Jesus Christ revolves entirely around blood covenant. Blood covenant is throughout the Bible. A better name for Testament is covenant. God will never alter His word or break a covenant He has made. Psalms 138:2 says *For You have magnified Your word above all Your name.* God's Word is His oath and He is fully capable of keeping every word He has spoken. We need to be people who keep our word. People of integrity and truth!

What are the Rewards of Integrity?

There is great reward for those who walk in integrity.

Proverbs 20:7 says *The righteous man walks in his **integrity**; His children are **blessed after him**.* Notice something here. If we are people who walk in integrity we will be blessed spiritually, mentally, physically, socially and financially. Not only are we blessed but our mate, children and spiritual children God has entrusted us with will also be blessed. What a powerful promise! The opposite, if we lack integrity and embellish the truth is to bring a curse on our life, our children's and those under us. For no other reason that should make us want to walk in integrity.

This is how we built this ministry into what we have today. I was brought up in a home where a strong strong emphasis was placed on integrity, honesty and hard work. God has greatly blessed us because integrity is of utmost importance to us in our personal lives and ministry.

From the early years of ministry, till 1998 I had many issues with pride, arrogance and insecurity. In those days I loved talking about myself and what Christ was doing through me. Giving Christ glory is one thing, but when we are trying to be the center of attention, watch out! He said He would share His glory with no other (see Isaiah 42:8). The focus has to be Christ, not us and what we have accomplished. It's what He has accomplished! Many love the limelight, preeminence and attention on themselves. We need to learn to live our lives for the audience of ONE, and making sure He gets the glory due His name.

Even though I did have these character flaws, I could never allow myself to lie and exaggerate as I knew this would bring reproach to my Lord and Savour. Thank God I have dealt with the pride and insecurity issues as best I can since 1998. Sharmila and I will continue to deal with character flaws as they come up, with humility and repentance.

How much does integrity mean to you? Would you be willing to lose friends because you are truthful, honest and walk in integrity rather than trying to put on a show and look good for them? That is one test to see if you are person of integrity or not. We need to quit trying to prove ourselves to man and find all our security in Him. *He who walks with* **integrity walks securely,** *But he who* **perverts his ways will become known** (Proverbs 10:9). If you are a person of integrity, word will get out that you are one who can be trusted. You will be put over faster by God and man rather than someone who perverts his way (is deceitful, lacks integrity or embellishes the truth).

When **pride** *comes, then* **comes shame;** *But with the humble is wisdom. The* **integrity** *of the upright will* **guide them,** *But the perversity of the unfaithful will destroy them* (Proverbs 11:2-3). Notice integrity will guide you. The word guide in the original

Hebrew means it will **transport you.** Integrity will take you far in this life and the rewards will be great in the life to come. It will be guiding force in your decision making process, to keep you on the right path.

Many people think that a humble person is someone timid, shy, insecure and someone who can not look you in the eye. But that is not the fruit of humility. It is the fruit of pride and arrogance. Many do not realize that when you exaggerate, or lift yourself up it is because of insecurity (See Proverbs 27:2). Insecurity is a byproduct of pride and arrogance and it brings with it shame (ref. Proverbs 11:2).

A righteous man **hates lying,** *But a wicked man is loathsome and comes to shame* (Proverbs 13:5). Lying, pride and arrogance bring shame. Many people do not set out to be deceitful but are insecure in who they are, causing them to embellish and eventually tell lies so others think more highly of them. Be secure in who Christ made you to be. We should be people who hate lying, exaggerating, pride, and find our security in Christ and live our lives for the audience of ONE. It will take us further in these last days than we could ever imagine. I know because we have witnessed this time and time again.

What good is lying and embellishing the truth? Proverbs 6:16-19 says *These six things the LORD hates, Yes, seven are an* abomination to Him: A proud look, A lying tongue ... A false witness who speaks lies, And one who sows discord among brethren. There will always be gossip, strife, and competition wherever there is lying and arrogance. How do we combat this? By being people of truth and integrity. These things God hates and they are an abomination to Him. *Lying lips are an abomination to the LORD, But those who deal truthfully are His delight* (Proverbs 12:22). When you are a person of truth you are His delight.

The truthful lip shall be established forever, But a lying tongue is but for a moment. Deceit is in the heart of those who devise evil, But counselors of peace have joy (Proverbs 12:19-20). Do you want to go far in life then be a person of truth and integrity. You will go far in this coming wave of the Holy Spirit. Get ready to be used by Him!

*But a certain man named Ananias, with Sapphira his wife, sold a possession. And he kept back part of the proceeds, his wife also being aware of it, and brought a certain part and laid it at the apostles' feet. But Peter said, "Ananias, **why has Satan filled your heart to lie to the Holy Spirit** and keep back part of the price of the land for yourself? While it remained, was it not your own? And after it was sold, was it not in your own control? Why have you conceived this thing in your heart? **You have not lied to men but to God.**"*

Then Ananias, hearing these words, fell down and breathed

*his last. So great fear came upon all those who heard these things. And the young men arose and wrapped him up, carried him out, and buried him. Now it was about three hours later when his wife came in, not knowing what had happened. And Peter answered her, "Tell me whether you sold the land for so much?" She said, "Yes, for so much." Then Peter said to her, "How is it that you have agreed together to test the Spirit of the Lord? Look, the feet of those who have buried your husband are at the door, and they will carry you out." Then immediately she fell down at his feet and breathed her last. And the young men came in and found her dead, and carrying her out, buried her by her husband. **So great fear came upon all the church and upon all who heard these things.** And through the hands of the apostles many signs and wonders were done among the people. And they were all with one accord in Solomon's Porch. Yet none of the rest dared join them, but the people esteemed them highly* (Acts 5:1-13).

A number of years ago I heard about woman pastor I knew of near Minneapolis, Minnesota, USA. She received an invitation to minister in Kenya. In order to go she had to raise a lot of money to send to two pastors for setting up her ministry. It took awhile to raise the funds but finally she raised the needed funds. She sent it over to the pastors and bought her plane ticket. A short time later she was on a flight to Kenya expecting a great time of ministry. When she arrived nobody was there to pick her up. She tried to find the pastors but was unsuccessful. She flew back home very discouraged over what happened and how people had given to help her go to Kenya but nothing was set up. As time went by some people found the two pastors with the money they had stolen from her and her supporters. They had suddenly with no warning both dropped dead. End of story. *But outside are dogs and sorcerers and sexually immoral and murderers and idolaters, and* **whoever loves and practices a lie** (Revelation 22:15). Not a good place to be!

I believe in these last days that there will be more stories like this, of Holy Spirit dealing with dishonest ministers and leaders who take the presence of God for granted, continue deceiving and lying. You can not lie to Holy Spirit continually and willfully and expect to walk away with nothing happening. The effects of this type of dishonesty cause the name of Jesus to be blasphemed. Reproach is brought on Christians and Christianity. We need to live above lying, hype, exaggeration, deception. We will be blessed in the long run if we do and help further the Kingdom of God on this earth.

Jesus said *you shall know the truth, and the truth shall make you free* (John 8:32). True and lasting freedom comes from knowing the truth of His Word, walking in that truth and with integrity.

CHAPTER 13

The Roots of False Doctrine

F alse doctrine can creep into the Body of Christ though a variety of ways and attitudes. Let's take a look at ways false doctrine comes about in the Body of Christ. A friend of mine sent me some thoughts regarding this book and how the religious spirit deceives many. I want to share with you what he said. *"I was thinking about you writing the book on **Religion or Relationship** and how it is the enemy of God. I personally think it is the greatest enemy of the church, its root purpose to deceive us into thinking we are embracing the truth when it offers only the counterfeit. There is a pull or attraction that the counterfeit offers or people would not take it. It offers something that the authentic does not. For example, a beautiful very realistic but expensive flower arrangement. You never have to water it and it* *doesn't go bad after a week, but there was no life in it, no fragrance, not as soft to the touch."* -Rex Eberle

Different Ways False Doctrine Comes In

1. Pride and arrogance. Trying to be the center with something new, all for the glory of man. I have seen over the years some people come up with new doctrine just to show they are on the 'cutting edge' of something great and come across with arrogance to show they know it all. Sometimes the desire is just to be different and to stand out. This mindset can push people towards false doctrine. So much false doctrine has its roots in arrogance and pride.

2. Unbelief! So many false doctrines have come out of unbelief and questioning God. Putting question marks where God put a period. How much false doctrine has come about over the years simply because believers in Christ did not want to take God at His word. Example: Jesus said *"Most assuredly, I say to you, he who believes in Me, the works that I do he will do also; and greater works than these he will do, because I go to My Father"* (John 14:12). Notice the period after this statement. There are times while ministering and quoting this scripture in our meetings where I can almost hear the people putting question marks on the end of that statement. Thoughts like *"How can we do greater works than Jesus?" "Isn't that pride and arrogance to*

think we can do greater works than Jesus?" No! It is pride and arrogance to question Jesus and put a question mark where He put a period. We need to take the limits off Him and believe what He says.

3. Building Doctrine on negative experiences. How many have come up with beliefs contrary to God's word because of what they are personally experiencing? This is not a good way to develop sound doctrine. It is called **Isogesis.** It is a focus on what I am experiencing, what I believe already and try to fit the Word into that belief. A lot of false doctrine comes from that mindset. The best way to operate is by **Exegesis.** Drawing truth from the Word with no preconceived ideas. That is the best way to build on sound doctrine. Smith Wigglesworth, a famous healing evangelist, saw many undeniable miracles during his ministry and a number of people raised from the dead. He had a famous saying *"If God said it I believe it! That settles it!"*

Steve C. Shank says in his excellent book **Schizophrenic God? Finding Reality in Conflict, Confusion and Contradiction** *"Many let experiences in life determine truth for them instead of settling Jesus knows the truth, tells the truth and reality is only found in Him. We can not understand God by personal feelings only."* Sometimes feelings are not in line with His Word and with reality.

The first person I prayed for to be healed of cancer died a few days later. I could have developed a doctrine on how God does not want all to be healed or why healing does not work. Instead I was determined to press in more to learn about healing. Why? Because I already saw healing was in the Word and in the atonement. Since that time we have seen many hundreds of people healed of cancer, leukemia and tumors. My son Jesse being one of those supernaturally healed of leukemia after being in a coma for a number of days, never to have it again.

It is unfortunate that for many people their experience becomes more important than what the Word says. Many because of arrogance come up with new revelations or doctrines because of those negative experiences. Their attitude is such that 'because of my negative experience this what is true,' changing what the Word says to fit their experience. To sum it up **they have exalted their negative experience over the Word of God.**

4. Not centered on Christ's theology and the finished work at Calvary. Not coming up to His standard or teachings but lowering beliefs to what you believe and experience. Holy Spirit dropped this in my spirit while writing this chapter. **Christ's doctrine and heart attitude is the barometer by which we measure or discern every doctrine and belief.**

One religious tradition that was passed down from misunderstandings of the of book of Job is the belief in physical suffering, which is called asceticism. It also came about because of the negative influence of Greek philosophy and what it brought into Western Christianity, by Augustine in 400AD. Because of that false teachings came out regarding **Paul's Thorn in the Flesh** during this time period. I address these false religious traditions of men in depth in my book OVERCOMING ROADBLOCKS TO HEALING.

Job was the first book of the Bible written, long before the time of Moses. Job said *The Lord gave, and the Lord has taken away; Blessed be the name of the Lord* (Job 1:21)." Job at that time may have believed that to be true because the of the negative circumstances he found himself in **(Isogesis).** But that did not mean that his doctrine was correct. Because of Augustine and John Calvin's teaching and beliefs (Calvinism) many believe God does both good and bad to us and we are not to question it. Job falsely accuses God of doing evil and oppressing him. Job 2:7 says *So **Satan** went out from the presence of the Lord, and **struck Job with painful boils** from the sole of his foot to the crown of his head.* We know that it was Satan who did this to Job, not God. Job did not know this. Never once did Job acknowledge there was a Devil or demons who were doing the bad things to him. He thought it was God afflicting him.

Then along comes Augustine. Augustine taught *"Nothing happens unless the Omnipotent wills it to happen"* and also said that someone suffering *"ought not attribute (his suffering) to the will of men, or of angels or any created spirit, but rather to His (God's) will."* This was totally contrary to early church leaders and the Bible. James 1:16-17 says **Do not be deceived,** *my beloved brethren.* **Every good gift** *and every perfect gift* **is from above,** *and comes down from the Father of lights, with whom there is no variation or shadow of turning.* Pretty strong words from James. **Do not be deceived!!! God is not the author of bad things in your life. Nor does he send sickness and disaster and say "this is how I show my goodness to you or teach you a lesson."** This doctrine came about because Job tried to build a doctrine on what he was experiencing. Augustine, Calvin and those who follow this kind of teaching ran hook, line and sinker with this false doctrine. This fit perfectly with Augustine's Greek Philosophy.

Let's look at the book of Job to see how this ends. God corrected Job's erroneous theology that He (God) was both afflicting and blessing him. So God spoke up and said *"Will you condemn me to justify yourself"* (Job 40:8 Moffat)? Job repented of his beliefs, forgave his friends also and God blessed him with twice as much (see Job 42:12). God was not Job's problem but on the contrary he was the answer or way out of

Job's problems or negative circumstances which many say only lasted about six months.

Look at how Augustine, a Greek Scholar brought so much false doctrine into Western Christianity. Much of it had to do with his personal negative experiences and with finding ways to fit his belief in Neoplatonism into his new found faith in Christ **(Isogesis).** The fruit of this brought about tremendous damage and took Western Christianity off course with what Jesus and early church taught. Steve C. Shank brought this out so well in his excellent book **Schizophrenic God? Finding Reality in Conflict, Confusion and Contradiction.** By far the best book I have ever read in my lifetime on this subject matter. You can also order this from our website: www.markandersonministries.com/product/schizophrenic-god.

5. Building doctrines because of offense. Teaching something different because of the way a certain expression treated them or acted. What I have seen some do is take a doctrine and with a spirit of rebellion go the opposite extreme to cut down a certain expression because they became offended. It could be because they were hurt or maybe because they saw someone who was 'wacky and extreme.' So their attitude is to throw the baby out with the bathwater. Many do this, go to the opposite extreme and end up in false doctrine.

6. Here is something about false doctrine I have seen over the years when following man more than Jesus. Then going into isolation or into a one stream of expression. It will cause many to walk in deception, arrogance and pride with a know if all attitude. I love learning from many streams to get a well balanced. I never will follow a man more than Jesus. Too many believers have and when the person they follow falls they fall with them. I have watched many Christian lives fall apart this way when the emphasis was the one man show or one stream. The ministers who go down this path in most cases are no longer accountable to anyone but themselves. The people who follow them are only accountable to that one minister or expression. They set themselves up for the fall along with those that follow them.

7. Another place where false doctrine has come about is when people follow someone who is greatly gifted say in miracles or the prophetic. Because the person they follow carries a strong anointing in their area of gifting they do not question anything, including doctrine that is spoken from that minister. I have watched way to many people over the years follow things contrary to God's Word simply because the person sharing that was greatly gifted. That is a dangerous place to go. We need to be like the Bereans. The Bereans did not just believe everything that was said. *These were more fair-minded*

than those in *Thessalonica, in that they received the word with all readiness, and* **searched the Scriptures daily to find out whether these things were so** (Acts 17:11).

In the area the prophetic there are many believers who use the prophetic wrongly to promote their own desires. They say *"I have heard from God."* What they are basically telling people is don't question what I say because *I heard from God.* So many believers have gone down a path of self deception because of this. Some believers are constantly saying this. All it takes is some examination to see that the words they are giving are not coming to pass or maybe somehow God changed His mind for this person and now He is saying something different. We will call it for what it is. It is a religious spirit and the religious spirit seeks to control people.

Be very careful in saying *I heard from God.* Don't be ashamed to say you heard from God when you really do. But learn the difference between the Holy Spirit speaking or religious spirit speaking. If it is Holy Spirit He will never contradict the Word of God, promote selfish desires or use the prophetic to control people. Because He will always lead us into all truth (See John 16:13).

8. Picking and choosing beliefs that fit one's selfish desires. False prophecies are usually used to bring this about. Many will

either say the Lord told me this. That way nobody questions them, because after all the Lord spoke to them. Or they run to meetings where someone will give prophecies that tickle the ears or prophecy what they want to hear, causing them to plunge even deeper into a false belief. Many you could say are led astray by the idolatry of their heart.

Many wonder when they walk in this kind of deception, why their prayers are not being answered. James 4:3 says *You ask and do not receive, because you ask amiss, that you may spend it on your pleasures.*

9. Many believers will form doctrine based on their surroundings. Let me give you and example. Some believers are involved in politics and embrace certain beliefs based on the party they follow and surround themselves with. I have watched many Christians slip into political correctness to line up with the party they like. They have embraced and now somehow believe homosexuality and abortion are fine. Why? Because that is what their party believes. God's Word has not changed.

Hillary Clinton said on April 23, 2015 at the annual Women in the World Summit in New York City. *"All the laws we've passed don't count for much if they're not enforced. Rights have to exist in practice, not just on paper. Laws have to be backed up with resources and political will. And **deep seated cultural codes,*** *religious beliefs and structural biases have to be changed."* If believers do not wake up to what she is saying some day we will wake up to great persecution against Christians in this country, who believe in the Bible. Some of those leading the charge will be once committed Christians, who have become politically correct and no longer believe the Bible is God's infallible Word. That day is already here!

Other believers limit themselves to only fellowshipping with a certain expression in the Body Christ, thereby becoming very narrow minded in their beliefs. I love gleaning from many different camps in the Body Christ, as long as they are following what the Word of God says. Why? One reason is to keep free from deception. Imbalance can bring deception.

10. Where is the focus? This one is crucial to walking in freedom, truth and reality. Jesus said in John 8:32 *"You shall know the truth, and the truth shall make you free."* Where is your focus? Is it on your circumstances or on His Word? It makes all the difference whether you walk in freedom or you walk in bondage. Your focus needs to be His Word. That is what sets us free from bondage.

Paul said in Romans 1:16 *For I am not ashamed of the **gospel of Christ,** for it is the **power** of God to **salvation** for everyone who believes....* What is the gospel? IT IS THE GOOD NEWS OF

JESUS CHRIST! The good news of Jesus Christ is the POWER OF GOD UNTO SALVATION. In the Greek the word salvation means forgiveness, physical healing, deliverance, protection, to be made whole, and some cases prosperity.

1 John 2:8 says *the darkness is passing away, and the true light is already shining.* Focus! This is crucial, if we desire to see a lasting move of God and reap the end time harvest of souls. Are we focused on light or darkness? The good news of Jesus Christ or bad news? What God is doing or on what He has not done? The early church had their focus on a big resurrected Jesus. Even after being beaten and threatened their focus never shifted. *And they agreed with him, and when they had called for the apostles and beaten them, they **commanded that they should not speak in the name of Jesus,** and let them go. So they departed from the presence of the council, **rejoicing that they were counted worthy to suffer shame for His name.** And daily in the temple, and in every house, **they did not cease teaching and preaching Jesus as the Christ*** (Acts 5:40-42).

They focused on Jesus, His words and actions. Today, somehow that focus has shifted for many Christians. Many focus on what God has not done, or their problems or what the enemy (Satan or demons) is doing more than what Christ has done. When our focus is centered on what He has not done then the fruit of that focus becomes very obvious. It breeds unbelief and offense within the church that literally can stop the move of God (see Mark 6:1-6). Many problems develop in an environment like this.

In John 5:1-16 Jesus healed a man who had been crippled for 38 years. He was the only one healed by the pool of Bethesda among all the sick and crippled who were laid there. Also in Luke 5:17, *"and the power of the Lord was present to heal THEM."* Them always implies more than one. Yet only one crippled man was healed in Luke 5:17-26. As we read on, one can see that the religious leaders reasoned and were offended with Jesus (vs. 21). Could that have hindered Christ's miracle power? The religious spirit on a number occasions, along with offense held back the power of God from manifesting in their midst.

When similar miracles occur today you can be sure that the media and many Christians who are bound by a religious spirit and offense zero in on those who were not healed as opposed to rejoicing over the ones who were healed. Why do believers act this way? Because of a distorted focus! There were those in the Gospel accounts who were not healed. But the Gospel accounts zero in on those who received their healings rather than the ones who did not. Why? Because when we get GOOD AT THE GOSPEL, sharing the good news or testimonies of our GREAT BIG GOD it becomes the seed that reproduces miracles time and time again.

Many Christians permit the media or negative circumstances to be the lens through which they perceive God. Later when they require a miracle from God they wonder why they don't receive their miracle. They have lost track of what God has done and focus on what He has not done. Some get offended with God or His **ministers.**

Many years ago the Lord showed me that if I was offended or critical with a ministry or a certain emphasis in the Body of Christ then I would not be able to receive from them or the anointing on them unless I repented. I have seen the media and believers get easily offended with people like Benny Hinn for example. They zero in on a small flaw in his life or someone not healed under his ministry, ignoring the many who were.

The enemy knows that if we keep our mouths shut about what God has done then there will be no reproduction of those miracles. Isaiah 62:6 says *You who make mention of the LORD, do not keep silent.* The enemy loves to silence believers, get their focus off and keep them from sharing the testimonies of our great God. He wants us to focus on what he and his demons do more than what God does so he has an environment to keep working his destructive power. Sad to say many believers fall prey to these tactics.

When our focus is on what God has done Romans 10:17 says, *So then **faith comes by hearing**, and hearing by the word of God.* Faith and the power to act come into our hearts when we hear what God has done or is doing. It activates faith! It is sad that in many Christian circles there is no mention of the miracles Christ is doing, or pressing in for these miracles He longs to do in our midst. It breeds unbelief and reliance on natural abilities instead of faith in God which can activate His miracle working power.

If we act according to the Bible and focus on what God has done and is continuing to do it will get the momentum going for what He desires to do in the future. It's like getting on a long moving train. Once it starts moving one does not want to stop it or get in its way. Just keep that momentum building!

If we focus on the good things God is doing then that becomes the lens through which we see; or one could say it becomes our belief system. It becomes the way we perceive God and what He can and will do continually.

Preaching only a 'Heard Gospel'

The Great Commission was never meant to only be preached but to also be demonstrated with miracles, signs and wonders (see Mark 16:15-20). Words may draw some to Christ but unless many see the actual manifestation or visible power of God apathy can set in. Some may even turn from the faith. We need God's manifest presence in our midst and not excuses why His presence isn't manifesting in our midst.

In these last days much of Christianity has become content with just a heard Gospel. Many are full of head knowledge but no power. It is nothing more than a religious spirit that leads to arrogance also. *We know that we all have knowledge. Knowledge puffs up, but love edifies* (1 Corinthians 8:2).

In the days of the early church the preaching was always followed by miracles, signs and wonders, a HEARD AND SEEN GOSPEL. The early church when being persecuted said *For we cannot but speak the things which we have **seen and heard*** (Acts 4:20). They kept the testimonies of what Jesus was doing fresh in their hearts and minds and shared them over and over. They did not let a religious spirit rob them from keeping their focus on Jesus by caving to political correctness or watering down their message.

Look at Phillip in Acts 8:4-8 *Therefore those who were scattered went everywhere **preaching the word.** Then Philip went down to the city of Samaria and **preached Christ** to them. And the multitudes with one accord heeded the things spoken by Philip,* *hearing and SEEING the miracles* which he did. For unclean spirits, crying with a loud voice, came out of many who were **possessed** (Greek demonized); *and many who were paralyzed and lame were healed. And there was* **great joy in that city.** Notice the words *hearing and SEEING the miracles!* The early church was not just talk! A religious spirit is very good at talk but not the walk or demonstrating with the power of God.

I frequently share from Acts 8:5-8 in our India campaigns to let Hindus, Muslims and Sikhs know what happens when Jesus Christ comes to their city. I also share what He did in the Bible, and in other campaigns we have held in India. I tell them He will do the same in their city. Sure enough the same miracles flow strongly from the first night onward and great joy comes to these cities.

In August 2007 **Randy Clark** prayed for impartation over me in Castle Rock, Colorado. I did not feel anything but received it by faith. Prior to this prayer for impartation we were already seeing many mighty miracles in our outreaches around the world. But things quickly were taken to a whole new level. A short time later our daughter Charisma and her friend saw an angel two stories tall walking through our home. A short time after that we left for India. Sharmila will share with you what transpired there and has now become a regular occurrence in our outreaches in Northern India ever since 2007.

HINDUS & MUSLIMS SEE & HEAR JESUS!

Fall 2007 Report by Sharmila Anderson

"Many times I find it extremely difficult to express in words the power, compassion and mercy of Jesus Christ. Our outreach in **Moradabad, India** *was one such time. I will to try my best to describe what happened there as Jesus tangibly revealed Himself to many Hindus and Muslims.*

Prior to our departure for this outreach Mark had mentioned that he sensed that this trip would be a turning point for the ministry in India, that something powerful was about to break forth!

We conducted a 5-day city wide, open-air campaign in Moradabad October 23- 27, 2007. During this period approximately 11,500 people decided to become Jesus' followers, by surrendering to His Lordship, and many hundreds were healed of all kinds of ailments. Many of the people who testified of being healed said they either audibly heard Jesus' voice, or saw Him face to face, or saw angels. One gentleman said he saw thousands of angels all over the campaign grounds.

From the first night we knew that Holy Spirit was pouring Himself out on hungry Hindus and Muslims, as many testified of being healed. Most did not get the opportunity to testify of their healing as it was getting very late and the meeting had to be closed down. By the final night, over 9,000 people had gathered, hungry to hear about Jesus. Many of them for the first time in their life.

On the first night **Mukesh Kumar** testified that during prayer for healing he told Jesus "if you are real I want to experience you." Immediately he felt warmth in his body followed by coolness, and then a strong current went through him, after which he was fell to the ground. He arose knowing that Jesus was the true God and decided to follow Him.

Momine, a young Muslim boy had no blood circulation on one side of his face, as a result of which he could not blink his eye. The Lord touched him and he was able to blink his eye and speak clearly.

Vandana sat alone at the far end of the grounds. When we had people come forward for mass healing prayer she remained, sitting alone in the darkness. She suffered with seizures, asthma and was mentally tormented. During the mass healing prayer she saw someone walk towards her from the crowd. It was Jesus. He walked up to her, touched her, told her that that everything will be OK and she was healed.

Sunil Massih saw Jesus in the midst of the crowd along with thousands of angels. He said that one of the angels touched him.

Vineet Kumar, 12 years old, suffered with severe pain in his lungs. He testified that someone touched him and he heard an audible voice say to him, "son you are healed! Go up and testify." This young boy was extremely charged. He began to boldly praise Jesus in front of the huge crowd.

These are just a few of the healings that occurred. The blind saw, the deaf heard, cripples danced for joy, tumors dissolved, the demonized were set free, and individuals on their death beds were healed. THE POWER OF GOD WAS PRESENT TO HEAL. Many people testified that they literally **felt a presence reach into their bodies, pull the sickness out of them or put body parts back in place.**

Neelam - Was dying. She suffered with jaundice (swollen liver) and was bedridden. Jesus walked through her bedroom walls and appeared to her. He reached over and caressed her in bed, telling her to go the campaign and she would be healed! She came out to the campaign. After prayer she testified of her miraculous healing! It is really a good meeting when you have Jesus going door to door telling people to attend the meeting, because He would be showing up to heal many. You can not work up that kind of scenario. It's totally a grace thing.

The news of the campaign spread to surrounding towns and by the final night people had come from great distances to receive healing from Christ. The local television station covered the campaign, *which was good publicity for us. Articles about the campaign, Jesus healing people and Mark's message appeared in newspapers too.*

We have heard that on the Sunday after the campaign each church added an average of 5-6 new families. Healing testimonies continue to flow in. The pastors are determined to disciple all the souls harvested during this campaign. The media in Moradabad said that THE TRUE GOD HAS VISITED OUR CITY AND HAS SHAKEN IT!"

Now in our outreaches wherever we travel we share of His ongoing miracles and He repeats the very ones we talk about time and time again. It now has become a regular occurrence for Jesus or angels to appear to people, or for people to feel an invisible hand ripping sickness out of their bodies or putting body parts back together.

Revelation 19:10 says ... *For the* **testimony of Jesus** *is the* **spirit of prophecy.** Our focus has been the testimonies of Jesus rather than things that have not occurred yet. Why? When we focus on what He is doing and share about that it has prophetic power to foretell the future, that He can and will repeat the same miracle. *God shows personal favoritism to no man* (Galatians 2:6). If He does it for one He will do it for all. That has to be our focus!!

John 21:25 says *And there are also many other things that Jesus did, which if they were written one by one, I suppose that even the world itself could not contain the books that would be written. Amen.*

1 Corinthians 2:4-5 says *And my speech and my preaching were **not with persuasive words of human wisdom,** but in **demonstration** of the Spirit and of power, that your **faith should not be in the wisdom of men** but in the **power of God.*** Paul said he came demonstrating the gospel. His emphasis was God confirming the word he preached. The emphasis was more on seeing God move rather than eloquent words. People bound by religion many times have eloquent words but no power to back them up. Notice his mention of words of human wisdom and wisdom of men.

Much emphasis today in the Body of Christ has been on what comes naturally to us. If our walk with Christ has become that way (predictable) we need to cry out to God and learn to depend upon Him even more to accomplish things way beyond our natural abilities. Jesus said *I am the vine, you are the branches. He who abides in Me, and I in him, bears much fruit; for **without Me you can do nothing*** (John 15:5). If our dependence is on Him we will be brought out of our comfort zone and see a move of God that will draw the unsaved.

Has the Body of Christ learned to rely too much on natural ability and is that keeping us from seeing God's manifest presence in our midst? The early church preached the Gospel of Jesus Christ that truly was good news to those living in hopelessness and despair. Was it politically correct? No! Many died as martyrs for their belief in and testimony of Jesus Christ. It did not prevent the early church from moving forward. They kept their focus on the gospel (good news) of Jesus Christ. In spite of great opposition they turned their world upside down with a gospel message that was not only preached or heard, but was seen as well. Acts 17:6 says ...*These who have turned the world upside down have come here too.*

Gungun (small child) - had a hole in her heart. Felt a hand touch her and felt lightness.

Preety - had pain in eyes and family problems. Lord spoke to her "all your problems are gone."

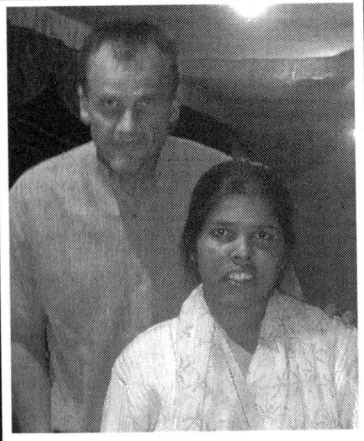

Vandana - Jesus appeared to her saying "you will be OK." She had suffered with asthma and epilepsy.

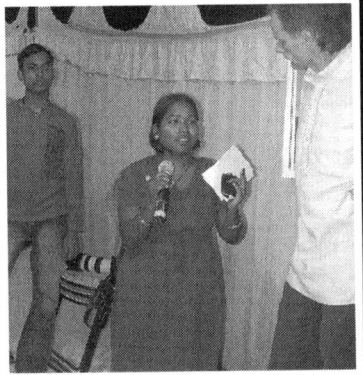

Neelam - Suffered with Jaundice (swollen liver) and was bedridden. Jesus appeared to her and caressed her while in bed telling her to go the campaign to be healed! Testifies of her healing!

Moradabad, India outreach

Vimla - Head had not healed after a brain operation. There was a gap in her head and a bone was out of place. She felt the presence of the Lord; was completely healed. Could hit her head with no pain.

Victor - Was very sick, unable to walk, had family problems and was depressed. He believed he would be healed at the campaign. His family mocked him for wanting to go and would not take him to campaign. Jesus healed him of everything.

Rajendra Prasad - Had 3 broken bones in arm! Healed by Jesus!

Prabha - Came to the stage in tears! Was blind! Saw a bright light and her eyes were opened!

Moradabad, India outreach

12 year old **Vineet** - Had pain in lungs! Holy Spirit touched him and Jesus said "son you are healed, go up and testify!" He immediately came and started boldly testifying what Jesus had done.

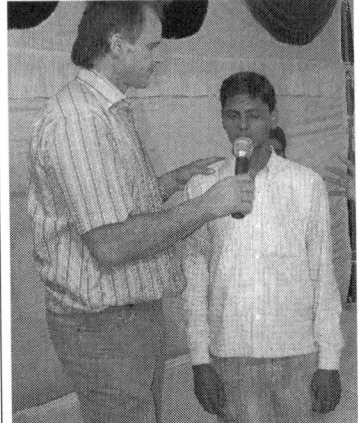

Momine - Had no circulation in right side face, could not blink his eye or speak clearly. After prayer in Jesus name, completely healed!

Many gather to hear about Jesus - In first ever citywide open air campaign in Moradabad, Uttar Pradesh, India. 11,500 turned to Christ in 5 days.

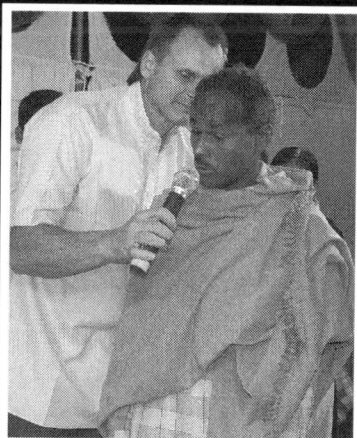

Prem Lal - Deaf and blind - 6 years! Healed by Jesus!

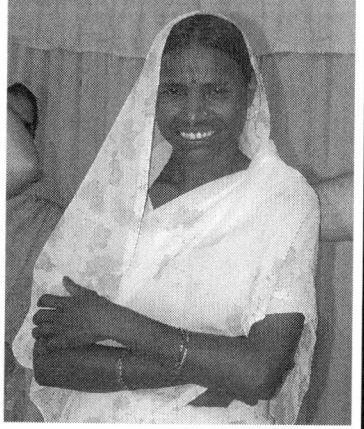

Santosh - Had manifested with demons starting the first night. Found freedom in Christ the last night.

On the final night our custom is to have all the participating pastors introduced so the many who came to Christ would go to their churches. During the first Sunday after the campaign each church averaged 5 to 6 new families. Now churches began following up those who filled out decision cards.

Moradabad, India outreach

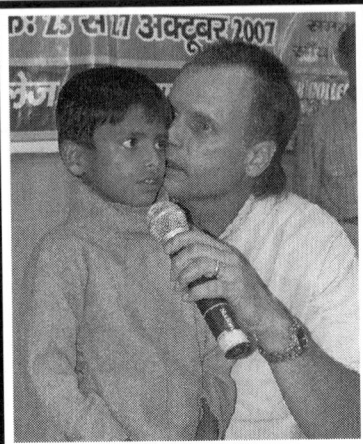

Reshab - Hears and speaks for the first time in his life after healed by Christ.

Shankar - Felt a hand pull the sickness out of his body.

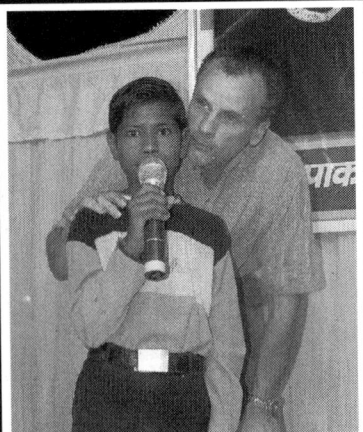

Arvind Kumar - Was deaf! Now hears after Jesus opens his ears!

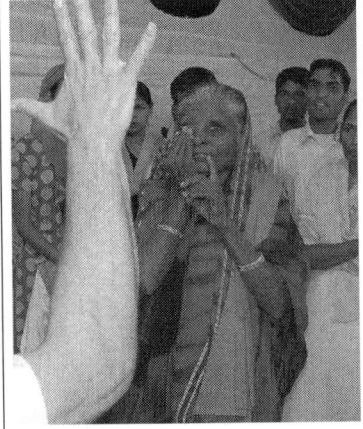

Guddi - Had a blind eye and tumor on elbow! Healed by Jesus!

Moradabad, India outreach

Mrs. Kaddy - Suffered with cataracts, diabetes and was crippled. Healed by Jesus!

Alice - Blind and body racked with pain! Healed by Jesus!

Ganbahadur - Was paralyzed! Now dances for joy after Jesus healed him!

Kallu - Was deaf, had poor vision, and an ulcer all healed by Jesus.

CHAPTER 14

Restoring America's Christian Heritage and the Damaging Effect of the Religious Spirit in Politics

An Important History Lesson Part I

July 9, 1755 was a crucial day in USA history. Our fragile nation hung in the balance. It was during the French and Indian War that a 23 year old colonel was fighting alongside the British commanding 100 men from Virginia. This man was a strong believer and follower of Christ. When marching to the enemy fort, Fort Duquesne (now the city of Pittsburgh) they were ambushed. The French had Indian snipers who were hidden in the woods, rocks and logs who were ordered to shoot and kill all the mounted officers so that the rest would be massacred or flee. Their plan worked and most of the army was wiped out with many more wounded in this battle. This young colonel bravely rode up and down the battle lines risking his life. He was shot at 17 times by expert marksmen, one of whom claimed he never missed. When word got back to Fort Cumberland that is was a massacre, hope was lost. They heard this young officer was dead.

Eight days later on July 17, 1755 this young colonel and all his troops arrived back to Fort Cumberland unharmed. Here are the words of this young colonel *"I now exist and appear in the land of the living by the miraculous care of Providence that protected me beyond all human expectation."* He recounted how after battle he took off his vest. There were **four bullet holes in his vest and not a one penetrated his body. Horses were shot out from under him, yet he survived.**

This young colonel was quoted as saying *"I have only been an instrument in the hands of Providence."* Word spread quickly of this young officer and of God's (Providence) intervention in this battle. Rev. Samuel Davies was considered to be the best preacher of those days. He began to share of this divine moment in our nation's history. As result the **first Great Awakening hit the shores of America and revival broke out. This story of God's intervention was taught in our public schools for next 150 years until those who wanted God removed from our history were able to remove it from our history books.**

In 1770 the old warrior chief who shot at him and told his young warriors to also shoot at him in that battle, had a chance to meet this colonel. This chief after seeing many shots taken at him to no avail, told his warriors to stop shooting. Here is what he said about that day. *"I have traveled a long and weary path that I might see the young warrior of the great battle. (I am) come to pay homage to the man who is the particular favorite of Heaven, and who (can) never die in battle."*

This chief also prophesied and said *"I am come to pay homage to the man who is the particular favorite of Heaven, who can never die in battle. Who in one day will lead a great nation."* And just who is this man? The first president of the USA, George Washington.

Many who want to rewrite our history have called this president and most of our early founders deists. What is a deist? A deist is very similar to an agnostic, someone who believes in God but believes He is far removed from the daily affairs of man. Sad to say many Christians have brought into those lies by getting their information from prejudiced sources, people bent on getting God out of our country and politics. Two excellent books that refute George Washington being a deist are **George Washington's Sacred Fire** by Peter A. Lillback (National Best Seller -1187 pages) and David Barton's easy to read mini book

America's Godly Heritage. You can order **David Barton's** book from our website: www.markandersonministries.com/product/americas-godly-heritage.

Many because of the continuous effort of those who are trying to erase or distort our Christian history do not know how the Declaration of Independence and US Constitution came about. There existed tremendous contention among the forefathers as they penned the Constitution so Ben Franklin, a strong believer called a prayer meeting. The Constitution came about from days of prayer and seeking the face of God. **President John Adams one the signers** said *"The general principles on which the fathers achieved independence were the general principles of Christianity. I will avow that I then believed, and now believe, that those general principles of Christianity are as eternal and immutable as the existence and attributes of God."*

When George Washington became our first president, as he was sworn in, he placed his hand on the Bible and said *"So help me God."* From there he immediately along with many other framers of the Constitution went down to what is today ground zero in New York City and had a prayer meeting at St. Paul's Chapel to give our infant nation over to the care of Almighty God. This great nation we love, came about when godly men sought God's face in prayer. George Washington wanted to continue that practice when he became our first president. By the way St. Paul's Chapel withstood the 9/11 attacks and still stands today as a symbol of our great Christian history.

Looking at America today, who is to blame for all the turmoil and chaos spreading within the country? I personally believe we preachers, pastors, priests and Christians are to blame. It is almost like we have taken for granted what our godly forefathers passed on to us and shed their blood for. I'm a part of that. Before you get mad at me hear me out. The ministers in the late 1700's were called the **Black Robe Regiment** by the British. The British saw the American pulpit largely responsible for the American independence and government. They were courageous and patriotic. They greatly influenced and made this nation so great. They trained soldiers for the military during the time of the revolutionary war. The British targeted these ministers more than any others because of their great influence.

Today most Christians and ministers love a non-confrontational lifestyle at all cost. But on the other hand the Apostle Paul talking about the last days said *Yes, and all who desire to live godly in Christ Jesus will suffer persecution* (2 Timothy 3:12). There are many promises in the Bible that we like to claim. I'm sure not too many want to claim this one. I tend to believe we will not have a choice in the days to come.

We need to stand for something or we will fall for nothing. I am all for peace, the blessings and claiming the promises of God but there will be times we will be confronted to make a stand and go against the grain like our early founders did if we want to take this nation back for Christ from evil men and women controlled by demons. They want to rid our country of God and will do anything in their power to reach this demonic goal. The religious spirit seeks to comply and blend in when we are called to make a strong stand for Christ. Don't give in!

It was mostly clergy who were responsible for the Declaration of Independence and the Constitution. The first amendment reads *"Congress shall make no law respecting an establishment of religion or prohibiting the free exercise thereof."* Please notice there are **no words in the amendment such as separation, church or state.** The reason for this amendment was so there would be no state religion like England had but on the contrary people were free to worship and believe in God as they desired. This spoke how our country was founded, much more on relationship with God than religion. For 175 years America followed and embraced this amendment in our schools and throughout society. Eventually America bought into a lie in 1947 that said there is a separation of church and state. I will show you just how much damage this produced in America. I believe we, with true Christlike humility (and not what society thinks is humility) can take back this nation. Let me share with you why I make these statements. First we will look at true and also at false humility, then the separation of church state lie and how it has caused this nation to go down a dark slippery slope.

Why Humility? Part II

*If **My people** who are called by My name **will humble themselves,** and pray and seek My face, and turn from their wicked ways, then I will hear from heaven, and will forgive their sin and **heal their land*** (2 Chronicles 7:14). The word humble means to get low or be in a bowed position. The George Washington painting at Valley Forge portrays this probably the best. He was a leader totally dependent on God, who was given to much prayer. He knew what it was to get low and serve this great nation.

This simple verse holds the key to America's future. Which way will America go? First of all notice God says *"if my people."* Notice he does not say if the Democrats, Republicans, the president, progressives, atheists, Muslims, Satanists or the ungodly repent. **"If my people!"** The first thing He says to do is HUMBLE THEMSELVES. I believe there is reason the humbling comes first. Without true humility the prayers, the seeking His face and healing of the land and other things do not fully take place.

Though the LORD is on high, Yet **He regards the lowly; But the proud He knows from afar** (Psalms 138:6). Without humility lasting change does not come to the land. Once we posture ourselves in humility then comes the praying, seeking His face and turning from our wicked ways. Notice the outcome, a direct line from heaven to earth is open. Heaven comes to invade earth. Our sins are forgiven and our land is healed. Not only is it healed but it becomes a place where miracles, healings, signs and wonders can take place on a regular basis like it did for the early founders of this country.

Greek Philosophy and Western Christianity

With Christlike humility in mind let's look at the negative influence Greek philosophy has had in western Christianity. When Greek philosophy became intermingled with our western form of Christianity it brought about a false humility and taught us poverty is a byproduct of humility, that we should desire. It also began to shape most Christians and the world's thought of what it was to be humble. Many think humility is someone who is insecure, timid, shy, weak, simple minded, not influential, someone who will not accomplish much in this life time, etc. Why? Because their focus is mostly the spiritual realm and the afterlife.

By humility and fear [Hebrew: reverence] *of the Lord are riches, honor, and life* (Proverbs 22:4). Christlike humility brings the byproduct of riches, not poverty or a poverty mindset of accomplishing very little in life. Christlike humility has the ability to attract wealth, not for the sake of being wealth consumers but wealth generators for the sake of expanding the Kingdom of God. We have a choice to either believe religious tradition or the Bible. Which will you embrace?

How the Poverty Mindset Originated

Much of western Christianity was and still is greatly influenced by Greek philosophy starting around 400A.D. with Augustine, who was a Greek scholar. Some of it has been passed right down to present day Christianity and our western way of thinking. Much of it is religious traditions of man, making the Word of God of no effect (see Mark 7:13). It affects our Christian belief system negatively and goes completely against true biblical teaching. The belief that "the poorer you are, the humbler you are" has much deeper roots than many could ever imagine, and it has affected the Body of Christ and nations in such a detrimental way. As followers of Christ, we need to impact areas of family, government, media, entertainment, education, business, and much more if we are to make disciples and impact nations. If we operate from a poverty mindset we will not accomplish much in life.

The Greek philosopher Plato taught that there was a distinct separation between the spirit world and the physical world. I personally do not buy into this! Augustine was greatly influenced by Plato and Greek Philosophy. He studied in depth Neoplatonism, the reworking of Plato's philosophy.

During the Dark Ages, some Church leaders took oaths of poverty and chastity (abstinence from sex) because they believed (as many do today) they had to separate the spiritual from the physical world. They also believed in asceticism (physical suffering) and gnosticism that said if something felt good it could not be of God. That is the reason for oaths of poverty, chastity and asceticism, to be more spiritual. Other gnostics (agnostics or deists) focused on the physical world and, because they believed God was so far away, uninvolved in our lives and people could never get close to Him, they said, "Go ahead; eat, drink, and be merry. If it feels good do it!"

Neither way of thinking is biblical. In creation God made it all good, both the physical and spiritual realms. For Jesus and the early Church Jews, there was no separation of the spirit and the physical realm. They did not just focus on spiritual things. There was no secular/sacred divide. Work, worship, being involved in politics, and even sexual relations between a husband and wife are both spiritual, mental and physical, and they are good if do not separate the two realms like Plato and Augustine did.

Governments and the physical realm need to be impacted for and by Christ or nations will fall to the ones with evil plans. We cannot impact governments with a poverty mindset and false humility that listens to the advice of the ungodly. The ungodly political leaders, along with the bought for media, Hollywood and our present legal system tell us, *"There is a separation of church and state, so Christians should not be involved in politics."* Many Christians, especially ministers, buy into that lie.

Augustine focused mostly on the spiritual because that is what Greek philosophy taught was reality. Greek Philosophy taught the spiritual realm does have preeminence over the physical realm. This is true! But do not go so far as to separate the two realms like Greek philosophy and Augustine taught us to do.

Hosea 4:6 says *my people are destroyed for lack of knowledge.* Jesus never taught about a separation of the spiritual and physical realms. Nor is there a separation of church and state in the constitution or in the first Amendment of the United States. When we minister from our pulpits, saying that we should just keep everything spiritual, we keep the Body of Christ from impacting government and legislation. This is a poverty or religious spirit mindset at work. It keeps us from influencing society with the various giftings that God has put in the Church. The destruction of America or any society follows as Christians avoid impacting the physical realm, government, legislation, business, and the public square.

The religious spirit drives many Christians to think that if something is not spiritual, then it really cannot be from God. Contrary to Greek philosophy and what Augustine modeled there is no separation between the spiritual realm and physical realm. God wants the spiritual realm to be invading the physical realm. But if the Christians are trying to be super spiritual and trying to avoid the physical, we will never partner with the Holy Spirit and enable Him to (through us) invade the physical realm. Christ needs vessels to impact the various realms of society. We have to get outside the church walls to do this. We really can walk in the spirit and still impact the physical, while relating to and working in the physical realm.

The Separation of Church and State Lie

David Barton in his book America's Godly Heritage brings out how America has drifted from it's Godly Heritage. For 175 years there was no separation of church and state. Then in 1947 a court ruling was made where a part of President Thomas Jefferson's letter to the Danbury Baptists in 1802 was completely twisted and taken out of context in a court of law to say the exact opposite of what Jefferson and the First Amendment says and even worse the American public believed it. It ended up bringing in what we know of today as "the separation of church and state" lie. From there America starting going down a dark path believing a lie. Little by little getting God out of the equation and government more into being the answer.

Dr. William James (the father of Modern Psychology) said *"There is nothing so absurd but if you repeat it often enough people will believe it."* That's exactly what happened with insertion of the separation of Church and State lie in 1947.

An excellent book on how the Separation of Church and State came about is **Ten Tortured Words** by Stephen Mansfield. In 1947 a God-hating judge who worked at one time as lawyer for the Klu Klux Klan brought about the ruling on separation of church and state that many quote today. This happened because of false humility, while the church fell asleep and just stuck to its own little corner, so as not to rock the boat.

Today the modern day courts often quote the 1947 court ruling (separation of church and state) rather than abide by the Constitution. Many generations since have been brought up believing a lie because it has been repeated so often. David Barton states that at that time *"only three percent of Americans professed no belief in religion... Ninety seven percent did believe.* Yet the court ruled *and the three percent becomes the standard by which the rest of the nation (i.e.. the ninety seven percent) must conduct its public affairs."* The 3% began to slowly decimate our Christian heritage once they were given power, to create a huge divide in America, where now Christian principles are frowned on and it has progressed unchecked since then.

Realize when our government begins to muzzle the Christian voice and then it gets to the point the Christian view is no longer welcome in government we are heading into perilous times. This becomes the place where our religious rights will be stripped away and we will be forced by government to do things contrary to our Christian beliefs. It's already here! We have to wake up and rise up. That is not what America was founded on. We need to quit letting the minority (the God haters) dictate to us what this country should be like, all because we take what we perceive to be humility, a backseat in politics and let evil call the shots.

Now bring in the mindset of Greek philosophy into western Christianity with a distortion of what true humility is. Rather than take a courageous stand against the **1947 Separation of Church and State and 1962 removal of prayer court rulings,** and what the government is doing today, ministers and Christians said we just need to be humble and focus on spiritual things. Over the years I have heard ministers say we should not get involved with politics because after all there is a separation of church and state and it might also affect our tax exempt status. By the way, the tax exempt status was Lyndon B. Johnson's doing in 1954 while in congress to get the church off his back and win in a corrupt election process. Later he went on to be President of the United States of America. His tax exempt status scare has never been carried out even when brave pastors broke that law in recent years.

Congressman and Speaker of the House Paul Ryan is a strong believer in Christ who has gleaned much from David Barton. He wants to do away with the 1954 Johnson law so Christian ministers can have a voice in government once again. He needs a Republican President to make this a reality. Donald Trump if elected President in 2016 said he will do his best to reverse this law, to once again give ministers a voice in government. The impact of this decision could end up being seen and felt around the world in a very positive way and greatly impact the end time harvest of souls.

Where is our backbone? This is not the courage Jesus displayed, nor our early forefathers who shed their blood to give us this great nation. Jesus said *"I am humble."* He was and still is HUMILITY IN IT'S PUREST FORM. He was told not to go to Jerusalem after He raised Lazarus from the dead because the religious leaders wanted to kill Him. What did he do? Conform to these wicked leaders so as not to rock the boat? Did he just give into political correctness. No! He boldly went to Jerusalem knowing he would be arrested, tried and killed by these religious leaders.

The byproduct of Christlike Humility is COURAGE! The German word for Humility is DEMUT. It literally means humility and serving with courage. A brave German Lutheran minister by the name of **Dietrich Bonhoeffer** made this quote *"Silence in the face of evil is itself evil: God will not hold us guiltless. Not to speak is to speak. Not to act is to act."* Because of his Christlike humility and courage he made a strong stand against the Nazi aggression in World War II and paid for that stand with his life. Great is his reward!

Who does not like living a comfortable lifestyle? I do! We have to be willing though to come out of our comfort zones when needed and stand up for justice and truth to prevail in this country once again. That means getting active to make a difference in this country. Be a voice for positive change even if the masses mock you.

Do you know how the word 'politically correct' came about? Bruce Porter is his book **9/11 Target** shares how it started. Quoting from Bruce's book **"political correctness" flourished during Josef Stalin's Marxist dictatorship in Russia to denote one who heels to the Communist Party line.** The term was originally minted by a party hack named Leon Trotsky to refer to the **"useful idiots" who mindlessly conformed to the Bolshevik Party line.** This rotting corpse was revived in the 1960s. New Progressive "community organizers" who imagined themselves as intrepid revolutionaries following in the steps of dictators and genocidal maniacs like Ernesto "Che" Guevara, Fidel Castro, and "Chairman" Mao. Under Josef Stalin's brutal regime, anyone who dared express an opinion differing from the "Party," or Comrade Stalin personally, could expect an unpleasant terminal experience before a firing squad or permanent exile to the mines of Siberia."

In recent years around this world many have died because of political correctness and if it is not dealt with soon sad to say many more innocent men, women and children will die. Do you notice for the most part how people who hate God, hate Christianity or are atheists are the ones who tote this political correctness theme? Look at many governments today. There is a diabolical scheme to remove Christianity from the USA and many other nations by controlling leaders with political correctness. It is sad that many Christians do not have the courage, backbone or desire to rock the boat, and instead allow their national leaders to for the most part to slowly remove God from the public square. If these governments did it too fast people would rise up. But they keep doing it slowly so they can keep plodding along until we are like the frog in pot, and after time the water is boiling hot and then it is too late.

One of our early founders, Patrick Henry said *"Give me liberty or give me death."* What has happened to the bravery, courage and yes the humility of our early forefathers who were willing to speak up for what was truth and willing to die for their beliefs in freedom, faith and liberty? They took a stand for something and handed us a great nation. Most people in this generation have stood for nothing in politics and may fall for anything unless we turn this ship around. There is a diabolical evil that wants believers to keep quiet so they can take control of this nation and eventually the world.

The influence of a religious spirit and an introduction to Greek philosophy, separating the spiritual from the physical has done great damage to our country. Augustine and John

Calvin's teachings have brought about passivity in the Body of Christ. It has caused many in ministry to cower to political correctness in the pulpits, which eventually spreads into the church, then the family and now society. The ungodly succeed because they are **PROACTIVE and most Christians are only reactive. *'Whatever will be will be'* attitude when it come to politics. Many do not react until the ship is sinking or has sunk when it comes to politics, education, business, arts and entertainment, media, etc.** That is when it is too late. Will we rise up and get proactive or continue to cave to political correctness in politics and in our churches? Will we stand by and watch America decline and let the ungodly control our society and eventually the world?

One problem we face in our country that greatly hinders proper government from being elected is a self righteous attitude amongst Christians in the country. It keeps us divided rather than uniting to make our voice heard. It also keeps Christianity from properly influencing society.

Speaking as a conservative and an evangelical, I will give you an example of a religious spirit and self righteousness at work during the 2012 election. A lot of conservatives are bound by what we call a religious spirit when it come to politics. How? Over 30 million evangelicals did not vote in the 2012 election.

One evangelist bound by a religious spirit did not like either candidate in the 2012 election so his goal was to get one million people who would write in votes for Jesus instead. The election was decided by less than 2 million votes. Jesus was not running and those religious votes of self righteousness were for naught. The wicked laugh at such stupidity, which helped hand them the country.

Don't complain if you do not like what you see in D.C., if you did not vote. You are part of the problem. A religious spirit like this evangelist had are part of the problem that is taking our country downhill into moral decline because they did not consider voting to limit evil.

Edmund Burke said *"The only thing necessary for the triumph of evil is for good men to do nothing."* He also said *"Nobody made a greater mistake than he who did nothing because he could do only a little."*

Many evangelicals are looking for a Pastor in Chief and not a Commander in Chief. They do not see the bigger picture. Don't forget that the USA is only 25% evangelical Christian. So we need to learn to get together with people who might not see eye to eye with us. That is where humility and the need for unity comes in. That does not mean we compromise our morals. Keep in mind we love the sinner but hate sin just like Jesus (see

John 8:1-11). If the evangelicals would simply put aside the arrogance, self righteousness, religious spirit and attitude that is it all about our needs we can end up with a great country and get something done. 25% of the country with the same focus can greatly impact this nation for the better.

We better unite Conservative Evangelicals or we get the country of our arrogant or apathetic actions when we have the power to make a difference in this nation. In this 2016 election the choice is clear. Hillary Clinton will take us further away from Christ and appoint ungodly supreme court justices. Donald Trump, though far from perfect will restore many Christian values and appoint conservative God fearing, America loving judges to the supreme court. **This is so very crucial to what becomes the law of the land.** A religious spirit will keep a Christian from voting for the right leaders to govern our country.

Many Democrats like President Obama and Hillary Clinton were greatly inspired by Saul Alinsky. Who was this man? He hated Christianity and shortly before his death said in a Playboy Magazine interview *if there is an afterlife, and I have anything to say about it, I will unreservedly choose to go to hell.* Playboy Magazine: *Why? ALINSKY: Hell would be heaven for me. All my life I've been with the have-nots. Over here, if you're a have-not, you're short of dough. If you're a have-not in hell, you're short of virtue. Once I get into hell, I'll start organizing the have-nots over there.* Not long after this interview he passed away in 1972, only 63 years old.

Alinsky's most famous work, **Rules for Radicals** was published in 1971. It talks about how to overthrow our republic and use chaos and never to let a good crisis go to waste. He also advocated civil disobedience (much like we are seeing today). He advocated deception and community organizing to destroy our republic and the Christian principles the USA was founded on. Here is Alinsky's dedication of his book **Rules for Radicals** *"Lest we forget at least an over-the-shoulder acknowledgment to the very first radical: from all our legends, mythology, and history... the first radical known to man who rebelled against the establishment and did it so effectively that he at least **won his own kingdom —**
Lucifer."*

One leader who he mentored and greatly influenced was Hillary Clinton. She will carry on with what he taught her if elected as President. Saulinsky put a strong emphasis on lying and deception to bring about change. Proverbs 29:12 says *If a ruler pays attention to lies, All his servants become wicked.*

There is a diabolical plan to remove God and Christianity from this country. What will we do about it? Generations to come will look at this time in history and ask what we did to stop this diabolical plan to rob America of it's Christian heritage. Did we sit back and do nothing or did we take a humble courageous stand like our early founders did?

It is time for believers to rise up with authority, boldness, miracles and humility like Jesus, George Washington and our early founders walked in and take our country back, to the Christian heritage our nation was founded on. Our nation's early leaders were not self serving. They were humble, full of integrity, courageous, not ashamed to admit their dependence on and relationship with Christ. We can turn this nation around for Christ if we rise up with humility and courage like our leader Jesus! 1 John 2:6 says *He who says he abides in Him ought himself also to walk just as He walked.* Statistics show in David Barton's book **Separation of Church and State** it is already happening in our schools and other places of society as believers are rising up to take this nation back.

Charles Finney was a lawyer who had a powerful baptism in the Holy Spirit, a divine encounter that caused him to discontinue his law practice and plead the cause of Christ. He was used powerfully to bring a great awakening to America in the 1800's. So many Christian ministers were inspired by this bold evangelist who was used to turn America upside down with the Gospel of Jesus Christ. I was inspired by him in the early days of ministry. Finney did not separate politics and Christianity. Here is an important quote of his regarding the believer's responsibility in politics. *The time has come that Christians must vote for honest men and take consistent ground in politics . . . Christians have been exceedingly guilty in this matter. But the time has come when they must act differently. . .* **Christians seem to act as if they thought God did not see what they do in politics.** *But I tell you He does see it - and* **He will bless or curse this nation according to the course they [Christians] take [in politics].**

Sometimes we think the choices for who is running for elected office are not the best. Don't take for granted the shed blood of our godly forefathers who gave us the right to vote and be involved in politics. Get informed. Sometimes we are not voting for someone as much as against diabolical evil, to limit evil in our nation. There are diabolical demonic plans for this nation. Satan and his demons use people to carry out those plans. Paul said *Lest Satan should take advantage of us; for we are not ignorant of his devices* (2 Corinthians 2:11). He said in Ephesians 6: 12 says *For we do not wrestle against flesh and blood, but against principalities, against powers, against the rulers of the darkness of this age, against spiritual hosts of wickedness in the heavenly places.* We do not have to go down that path.

There is a diabolical evil wanting to control political leaders in Washington D.C., this country and also the world. Billionaire Atheist **George Soros** is one who is controlled by demons. He has become the ultimate 'Puppet Master' over many nations and has propped up Barack Obama and Hillary Clinton. Because of his influence they are allowed to get away with many wicked things. **If we, the Church do not rise up we are headed for extremely dark days in the near future.** We need to get proactive in legislation and politics or we will begin to witness things so devastating and diabolical like we have never before experienced in this nation and around the world. **It is time for the Paul Reveres to ride again, to stand up and speak out against evil trying to take over our country.** If Christians make the right stand and right choices it can greatly impact the end time harvest of souls throughout the world for the better.

Proverbs 14:34 says ***Righteousness exalts a nation,*** *But sin is a reproach to any people.* We need to vote for righteousness. George Washington said ***"It is impossible to rightly govern the world without God and the Bible."*** Embrace leaders who will embrace Christianity.

For more on this please listen to my latest teachings on this subject entitled: **Restoring America's Christian Heritage.**

Just go to www.markandersonministries.com. For more on the negative Influence of Greek Philosophy on Western Christianity check out my book **Overcoming Roadblocks to Healing.** In Chapter 2, I deal with the negative influence of Greek philosophy as it pertains to Healings and miracles. You can order this online at www.markandersonministries.com/product-category/books. You can also order my 2 CD series **The Negative Influence of Greek Philosophy on Western Christianity** online at www.markandersonministries.com/product-category/audio.

CONCLUSION

In conclusion let's review a few things. In Part I, we covered how the religious spirit can progress in a believer's life and if left unchecked can eventually become a demonic stronghold, greatly hindering the move of God. In Part II, more important than focusing on demons, the religious spirit and religion, which is the enemy of God, is focusing on relationship with Him. We can enter into a living relationship with Father, Son and Holy Spirit. As we place a strong emphasis on character (things like Christlike humility and integrity) along with the power of God we can experience a lasting move of God that will greatly impact eternity.

If the Body of Christ begins to understand that it is not about a religious charade to impress others but is all about Jesus and lost souls He died for then we can greatly impact eternity.

We need it burned in our hearts we are living for the Audience of ONE! We are not to live for the praises of men.

Sharmila and I are amazed that as we have taken on this attitude we have accomplished things we never imagined we could do. James 4:6 AMP says *But He gives us more and more grace [through the power of the Holy Spirit to defy sin and live an obedient life that reflects both our faith and our gratitude for our salvation]. Therefore, it says, "**God is opposed to the proud and haughty,** but [continually] gives [the gift of] grace to the humble [who turn away from self-righteousness]."* The humble get the grace! Grace will help you do things way beyond your ability. Miracles, healing, signs, wonders, favor, blessings, and so much more come by grace. You can not work many of these things up. You have to learn how to tap into grace. The humble and those who turn away from self-righteousness are candidates for the grace of God. Most of the things I am doing today were way beyond my ability but God's grace kicked in and took me to a higher level than what I could have ever accomplished in the natural.

Keep in mind the Father, Son and Holy Spirit primary desire is to have fellowship with us. Jesus did not come to birth a new religion but to bring us into relationship, fellowship and communion with the Trinity. From this connection we become carriers of His presence. *Though the Lord is exalted, He **regards the lowly [and invites them into His fellowship]; But the proud and **haughty He knows from a distance*** (Psalms 138:6 AMP). We draw near to Him by taking on His nature, HUMILITY (see Matthew 11:28-30).

It is time to rise up to the realm of God, come out our religious boxes and become all He is called us to be. Uncompromising balance and purpose can also help bring this about. Focusing on Christlike character, the authority we have in Christ, along with His power allow the world to see the real Jesus. In turn it brings about a powerful move of God that impacts cities and nations.

Time to go for it my friend! If this book has blessed you please spread the word about it and help others tap into the glory of God. Together we can usher in the great moves of God around this world, all for His glory!

Maan Bhadar Magar - paralyzed for 7 years. Carried to the campaign walks on his own after Jesus healed him during mass prayer - **Kohalpur, Nepal April 5, 2012.**

On the last day of **Kohalpur, Nepal** campaign many come forward during mass prayer for healing. Many were instantly healed as we waited on the presence of the Holy Spirit to move - **April 5, 2012.**

This man was ecstatic showing us his x-rays and medical records. He had been paralyzed in his upper legs and experiencing great pain in his lower legs. Instantly healed by Jesus - **Kohalpur, Nepal April 5, 2012.**

Maan Bhadari - One of many blind who received their sight back after Jesus opened her eyes. She had been blind for 12 years - **Kohalpur, Nepal April 4, 2012.**

Kamya 8 years old. Was born blind in her left eye. After laying hands on her she could see. Later that night she could not see out of her left eye. Kamya and her mother returned on the third night. I shared with them how to stand in faith for her healing. Then we prayed for her again, then she could see out of her left eye - **Ballabhgarh, Harayana, India, February 2014.**

Pastors and leaders who attended our 3 day training conference in Kohalpur, Nepal April 2012.

Manju - Traveled a great distance to come for surgery because of severe blot clot on uterus. Instead of going for surgery came to our meeting where Jesus instantly healed her.

House church meeting in Delhi, India. 200 people showed up for the service. 100 turned to Christ.

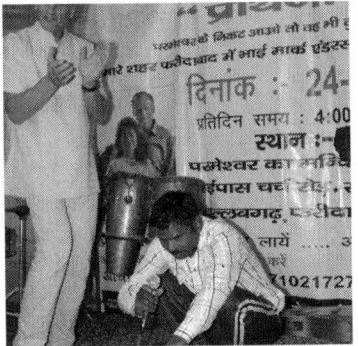

Munshi Lal - was in a severe accident 1 1/2 years ago. A metal rod was installed. He was in great pain and just asked the Dr about removing it that day. The cost was to much. During prayer time Mark said Jesus is dissolving metal, he was healed and came forward to demonstrate - **Ballabgarh, India February 25, 2014.**

BIBLIOGRAPHY

Overcoming the Religious Spirit revised edition. Copyright © 1996, 1998 by Rick Joyner quoted from part 1 Page 8 used by permission

Morning Star Publications & Ministries
P.O. Box 19409
Charlotte, NC 28219-9409
1-800-542-0278
www.morningstarministries.org

Quoted from Morning Star Journal article entitled **Prophetic Character** Copyright © by Rick Joyner used by permission

The Surpassing Greatness of His Power Copyright © 1996 by Rick Joyner Quoted from Chapter 17 page 195 used by permission

Quoted from an Article entitled **An Onslaught Against the Church** Copyright © January 1989 by Rick Joyner used by permission

The Final Quest Copyright © 1996 by Rick Joyner Quoted from part 4 page 102 used by permission

The Final Quest Copyright © 1996 by Rick Joyner Quoted from part 4 page 100 used by permission

Mark and Sharmila Anderson

Vision:

Reaching the unreached, telling the untold, churching the unchurched and training Christians to reach the unreached.

How:

Through open-air campaigns, ministry training conferences, women's conferences (with Sharmila Anderson), planting churches, supporting national ministry leaders, orphanages, literature, CD distribution and rock music.

Main Focus:

Rural and unreached areas.

Mark Anderson has been sharing the gospel, conducting campaigns, singing and planting churches since 1978. Over 200,000 people have already responded to Christ in his overseas campaigns. Churches have been planted from campaigns in India and Bulgaria. Mark has also helped pioneer churches in Canada and the United States.

Mark and his wife, Sharmila, travel together, fulfilling the Great Commission. Sharmila is also a very gifted teacher. Her main area of ministry has been training women to be all they can be in Christ.

To have Mark & Sharmila Anderson come speak in your area or for more information about Mark Anderson Ministries and a list of Mark's books and teaching CDs, please contact them at:

Mark Anderson Ministries
P.O. Box 66
Cody, WY 82414-0066 USA
www.markandersonministries.com
E-mail us at: goodnews@vcn.com
Phone: 307-587-0408

For other books by Mark Anderson, please visit their website:
www.markandersonministries.com/store

OVERCOMING ROADBLOCKS TO HEALING

Mark R. Anderson

Published by Apostolic Network of Global Awakening in 2012

Have you ever received prayer for healing or deliverance and nothing seemed to happen or you were healed only to lose your healing or deliverance a short time later? In this book we search out answers from God's Word to reveal things that can hinder healing. Clear cut answers from God's Word show how to overcome roadblocks to healing or deliverance.

Mark Anderson shares many things from his years of experience in the healing ministry. He explores major hindrances to miracles, healings and deliverance in western Christianity. Many Christians do not realize just how much Greek Philosophy influences their everyday Christian walk and belief system when it comes to healings and miracles.

In this book he explores what was Paul's Thorn in the flesh with scriptures and also examines the view that had it roots in Greek Philosophy. How to properly stand for healing, a miracle or deliverance is addressed. The final two chapters show how people like you and I overcame huge roadblocks to their healing and received their miracle from Jesus. You to can overcome the roadblocks to healing.

"Overcoming Roadblocks to Healing is an outstanding practical guide for those who are struggling to understand why healing does not come or last. At times, you may think the prayer of faith has failed or that you have done something to cause your sickness or pain to return. You may not know what to do next. I have been praying for the sick for many years. I have seen God do mighty things when praying for someone one time and then not see any results when praying for someone else another time. I have experienced victories and defeats in my own healing ministry and struggled at times with the mystery of why some do not get healed.

I believe Mark provides key insights from Scripture to help those who come against roadblocks in their healing. He not only offers strategy to get your healing, but gives personal experience where he has struggled to be healed or at times lost his healing. He tells you the truth about his struggle and the victory of overcoming his roadblocks to healing.

Mark exposes the lies that have caused believers to deny that healing exists or that it is not for today. He reveals the influence of Greek thought on our Western Christianity, which has caused a false belief that suffering and illness are the will of God for our lives. This misunderstanding has caused many to doubt that God can heal and their unwillingness to seek healing for their illness. Mark emphasizes that the truth of God's Word is the standard for which we should put our faith in. He stresses the need for believers to renew their minds by aligning thoughts and beliefs with the Word of God.

I believe this book should be read by every believer, especially those who need healing. It is a tremendous resource for those who have not walked in the healing ministry, to be aware of roadblocks in people's lives to healing. Thank you, Mark, for providing such a wonderful book that will help the church understand how to overcome the roadblocks to healing. "

– Randy Clark, Apostolic Network of Global Awakening

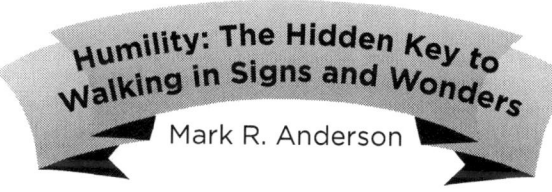

Humility: The Hidden Key to Walking in Signs and Wonders

Mark R. Anderson

Originally published by Destiny Image in 2010

Humility is the basis for spiritual and personal breakthrough—no matter your present circumstances. A fresh look at a trait that God welcomes and richly rewards.

As a teacher in the United States and to Third World countries, author Mark Anderson has observed first-hand how pride can destroy people and churches, while humility can revive and refresh people—and energize and expand even a fledgling ministry.

When pride comes, then comes shame; but with the humble is wisdom (Proverbs 11:2 NKJV).

Humility The Hidden Key to Walking in Signs and Wonders reveals the conflict between arrogance and humility and explores the fruits of this often-neglected but wholly vital virtue.

"The enemy would love for us to neglect humility because of its importance in ushering in the greatest move of God this world has seen," writes the author, who has spent 34 years sharing the gospel worldwide.

"This book helps you navigate your life between blatant pride and false humility helping you recognize what true humility looks like...The book is like a diamond in that humility is the diamond, and Mark helps us see all the various facets of the diamond, and there were many, all of which I found very helpful...

Humility the Hidden Key to Walking in Signs and Wonders, is the best book I have ever read on humility, and reveals the importance of humility's relationship to spiritual breakthrough, and revival."

– Randy Clark

YOU CAN TAP INTO CHRIST'S HEALING POWER

Mark R. Anderson

Published by Mark Anderson Ministries 2004

Miracles and healings do not have to be a rarity in your life or the life of any Spirit-filled or Spirit-led believer. By understanding your God-given authority and how to partner with the Holy Spirit, You can tap into Christ's healing power!

Christ made a show of the enemy openly. You can enforce what He accomplished

2,000 years ago. Sometimes faith is a fight. Learn how to stand for what rightfully belongs to you in Christ. Learn how your words shape and affect the way you live your life.

By understanding something that the children of Israel understood, you can create an atmosphere conducive for the Holy Spirit to move in power. You can literally affect the spiritual realm, releasing Christ's healing power in this physical realm. Learn the role humility will play in the healing ministry in these last days.

"Healing the sick was front and center in Jesus ministry. Mark Anderson has years of practical experience in seeing people receive miraculous healing through faith in Christ. His book You Can Tap Into Christ's Healing Power lays a foundation for healing and sets an atmosphere where miracles can easily be received. This teaching is for those who need healing for themselves, as well as for the one who wants to minister God's healing life to others."

– Evangelist Peter Youngren
St. Catherines, Ontario, Canada

Soul Winning: God's Heartbeat

Mark R. Anderson

Published by Mark Anderson Ministries 2000

Do you have the desire to reach the lost? Then this book is for you. It includes discussion of:

- Witnessing with a passion for souls
- Overcoming the fear of witnessing
- Successful evangelism keys
- Prayerful spiritual warfare and insight into the spirit realm
- Saying the right things at the right time
- The importance of follow-up
- Being a biblical witness with signs and wonders following

The Progression of the Religious Spirit

Mark R. Anderson

Published by Mark Anderson Ministries 2001

Jesus warned His close disciples of the negative fruit of the religious spirit. How much more do we need to heed the master's warning today and guard our hearts from an ungodly religious spirit? This book provides an in-depth study of Mark 7:1-13, including:

- How the religious spirit begins
- Finding fault: The first seed of the religious spirit
- Pride and false humility
- Holding onto man-made traditions
- Laying aside the commands of God

MARK'S MUSIC

Mark Anderson

COME

Words and Music by
Mark R. Anderson

www.markandersonministries.
com/christian-music/check-out-
marks-latest-song-come

I love these moments in time with you my sweet Jesus.

I love these moments in time. Come Holy Spirit.

We come with open arms to embrace you Heavenly Father.

Chorus

Come Father, Son & Holy Spirit (2X).

Verse 2

Teach us all ways Father, Son and Holy Spirit.

Teach us to worship you in Spirit and in truth.

Come in all your glory Father, son and Holy Spirit.

Chorus

Come Father, Son and Holy Spirit (2X).

38362720R00168

Made in the USA
San Bernardino, CA
04 September 2016